TOK

Diaspora Dialogues
presents

TOK

book 4
Helen Walsh, editor

Zephyr Press

Zephyr Press
170 Bloor Street West, Suite 804
Toronto, Ontario M5S 1T9
www.zephyrpress.ca

Library and Archives Canada Cataloguing in Publication

Tok / Helen Walsh, editor.

At head of title: "Diaspora Dialogues presents".
On cover: "Writing the new Toronto".
ISBN 978-0-9734112-6-3 (bk. 4)

1. Short stories, Canadian (English)—Ontario—Toronto.
2. Canadian poetry (English)—Ontario—Toronto.
3. Canadian fiction (English)—21st century.
4. Toronto (Ont.)—Literary collections. I. Walsh, Helen, 1965–

PS8237.T6T54 2006   C810.8'032713541   C2006-902670-X

Book design and composition by The Office of Gilbert Li
Copyediting by Madeline Koch
Cover illustration by Yarek Waszul
Printed and bound in Canada by Transcontinental Inc.

The paper used in this book contains 100% post-consumer fibre,
is acid-free, processed chlorine free, EcoLogo-certified, and was
manufactured with biogas energy.

Welcome to TOK, Book 4. In previous years, the short stories, poems
and plays in this anthology series were set in Toronto. This year's book,
while focusing primarily on the greater Toronto region, also includes work
commissioned from award-winning Montreal writer Rawi Hage, novelist
Jenn Sookfong Lee from Vancouver and spoken word artist Shauntay Grant
from Halifax.

The population of Canada is increasingly urbanized, with Canada's major
cities housing large and diverse populations working and creating together.
Yet the national dialogue on urban Canadian literature is in its infancy.
That should change over the coming years, so that Canadian writers who
want to be both internationalist and nationalist in their approach—using
their local environment as setting—will be encouraged to do so by the
publishing industry, and readers at home and abroad will have access to a
view of Canada that is urban, diverse and contemporary.

Work is selected for TOK on the individual merits of each piece, but it is
fascinating to see the accidental patterns that emerge when the collection
is read as a whole.

In writing "A Pair of Parades," Daniel David Moses was interested in
exploring the way memory and history work when one pictures history as
memory's spiral and not as history's progress—in creating another way of
remembering. His narrator listens to stories of his mother's participation
in early Santa Claus parades and wonders "how a Cayuga/Tuscarora Indian
girl ended up way back then in—I'm imagining—a red and round bounce of
a dress accompanying Santa's sleigh down University Avenue," interspersed
with his own memories of later times.

Memories and the past spiral for the father in Rawi Hage's story "Cough and Brume," as well, as the old man lies in a Montreal hospital bed, with the sounds of dying around him, his thoughts filled with the people and stories of his childhood in Lebanon, of a simple life in a contradictory land. Antanas Sileika's narrator yearns also for a more simple past, for a Toronto before the children of eastern European immigrants fled to the suburbs and their children, "aging Gen X hipsters and Gen Y moms with baby carriages," moved back downtown seeking "authenticity" and the latest real estate bargain.

Ghosts from the past—some more literal than others—float in and amongst these pieces. In Yvette Nolan's play, *Scattering Jake*, four friends scatter the ashes of a loved one around the city that he loved, accompanied by memories of the place he'd held in their lives. The ghost of a lost love from a previous generation challenges the acceptance of an inter-racial relationship in Sabrina Ramnanan's "The Iron Curtain." Anar Ali's narrator, haunted by a desire to return to an idealized past of his childhood in Kenya, takes his Toronto family into danger, refusing to acknowledge the changes that history and time have wrought. And in a poem by Tanya Bryan, her narrator gives a stranger on the streetcar a "two-fingered punk rock salute / as he takes the steps two at a time into the past."

Backward and forward. A record number of the stories in this year's collection use the eyes of children or teenage narrators to reveal the truths of the world around us. Sandra Tam's gentle story, "Ming Mei's Year," observes the changing seasons as they unfold, reflecting the impermanence of life and the inevitability of the common threads we find with others. Yiwei Hu parachutes her loyal communist narrator into a new city and a new family configuration. In both stories, Canadian apples play a central role.

The darker side of the city, of power and powerlessness, haunt Ken Babstock's astonishing poem, "Commissioners Avenue, Analysis Is the Poorer Half of Unknowing." Repairing torn roots, the body both worn down and buoyed up by ancient tides, and the "impossible metabolic rate" of the city swirl under and through Marge Lam's poetry.

Jen Sookfong Lee takes us on a psychogeographic tour of Vancouver in "Chill, Hush." From rental houses with peeling paint to big warm homes where parents pay attention to their children, from Vietnamese diners in orange-brick strip malls to hipster cafés, her teenage narrator rides the bus from East Vancouver to Main Street and beyond, riding away from a disintegrating family, wondering about her mother "if that fog that breathes with her is necessary because, otherwise, she would see what our life really is, which is the two of us together, thin and mostly silent."

The stories and poems and the play in this collection chart the effects of the environment on the emotions and behaviour of the characters and, by extension, on us as readers. They move us into a new awareness of our urban landscape, of our country and of ourselves. We're happy to be publishing these writers and hope you enjoy reading them.

Helen Walsh

No Longer
on the Menu
Antanas Sileika

I was surprised but not shocked when my Aunt Milda began to see her dead son up on the telephone pole outside her window in the mornings. At her age, anything was possible. I had to do something, and not just for her sake. As her tenant, I had everything to lose if she was carted off to a seniors' residence.

"I don't know how Frankie manages to perch there," she said when I came in from my heated garage to join her at morning coffee. "The wire is very thin."

As if that would bother a ghost. "The wire is immaterial," I said, humouring her, "like a line on a computer screen."

She didn't know what I meant and went on. "I call out from the window for him to come inside, but he never answers me. He just looks at me funny and then he disappears."

"You mean he vanishes into thin air?"

"I look away and when I look again, he's gone."

Aunt Milda wore her hair pinned up in the mornings, but her eyesight was poor and she was getting forgetful. A few wild gray wisps stuck out on one side of her head. She wore a beige housecoat and ate rye crisps with blackcurrant jam while she sipped camomile tea. Until a couple of years earlier, she had existed on chocolate and coffee, and now here she was, acting like someone's eastern European grandmother.

"Don't look so frightened," she said. "Remember, you're my designated favourite nephew."

It was an old joke that was supposed to buck me up, but it didn't work any more.

She meant no harm, but I was feeling sensitive anyway, and had been for a long time. I was glad my parents weren't alive to know I was staying in Aunt Milda's garage. Things had gone wrong for me a long time before, and she let me move in "temporarily." When the first winter came, I heated the garage with a leaky kerosene heater that stank so bad it made me gag. I got used to it.

As to the vision of Frankie up on the telephone pole, I believed Aunt Milda was working out her grief. She had barely had time to mourn the death of Frankie before her husband got sick, and then she was wrapped up in helping him die, so it was only natural that her son's ghost should appear now, when she had the time for him.

There was no one else left except the two of us, now three, if you counted Frankie; people died or moved away. Who else was she going to talk to? It made me wonder who I'd talk to after she was gone.

It also made me wonder where I'd stay after she passed away. The heated garage with the separate entrance onto the back lane had solved a lot of problems for me, but if she ever moved, I'd have to find new haunts.

"What language does Frankie speak to you?" I asked. "English or Lithuanian?"

"English."

I had been hoping to catch her out in a contradiction, to jolt her back into reality, but her answer was the right one. When Frankie was alive, he always spoke to her in English even though she spoke to him only in Lithuanian. I had thought she might be making him speak Lithuanian in the afterlife to compensate for his indifference to his ethnic heritage while he was alive. It's hard to make ghosts change their habits.

We were sitting in the combination living-dining room in her Dovercourt house, south of Dundas. Everyone else we knew from the old neighbourhood moved west forty years ago, first to Roncesvalles, then High Park and on to the suburb of Mississauga—for all I knew, the last of the old Lithuanian immigrants were still heading west. Maybe they'd meet the last Mohican somewhere around Saskatchewan. Aunt Milda had stayed as the district shifted, became Portuguese in the seventies, and then filled with young people.

In my day, the street used to be full of Ukrainians and Poles, but now it was leftover Portuguese, aging Gen X hipsters and Gen Y moms with baby carriages—a whole different generation, a whole different animal in the zoo.

The beautiful women in sunglasses didn't seem to come from anywhere at all. They were real estate cool hunters. They grew up in the suburbs, but now they wanted authenticity, and they came to look for it around Ossington and Dundas. The Annex and Little Italy were already too expensive.

Nobody cared about authenticity back in the fifties and the sixties. They had crawled out of the muck of their authentic villages and now, two generations later, their grandchildren were back, sniffing the air for traces of horse manure, herring and sheepskin.

If they ever smelled them for real, they'd call in the city health department.

The generation between these two, that would be mine, were embarrassed by their parents—the striving, the yearning, the sadness for all they'd lost were too exhausting a burden to take on. But my generation's kids seemed heedless and entitled. I could get whiplash by looking back and forth between the cramped meanness of the past and the cell phone–chattering future.

Except for a third layer of asphalt shingles, Aunt Milda's house hadn't changed at all for fifty years, maybe longer. The screen door was still wooden, with the netting torn in many places, the halls still painted in middling green so fingerprints wouldn't show.

Aunt Milda had given up dusting long ago.

"Why should I throw up the dust?" she asked. "It will just have to settle someplace else. For now, just let it be."

The living room used to be crowded with uncles, aunts and cousins over Christmases and weddings—the grownups dancing so hard that the floor bounced under their feet and the neighbours called to complain.

One of the ladies nicknamed "Little Fly" once got loaded and climbed up to dance on a table. This on-table dancing was some sort of big deal to them, though my aunt could never understand why dancing on tables was supposed to be such a sign of a good party. I couldn't bear to tell her that it was a big deal if the women doing the dancing were undressed, or at least scantily dressed.

Aunt Milda was old-fashioned in some ways, but she was modern in others. I loved her, both for herself and what she reminded me of, all the other ghosts in the room. Architecture and durable goods will leave remnants, something for archeologists to dig up in the future, but the actions that happened in the past leave nothing but memories in the rag and bone shop of my heart. How am I to preserve them?

Aunt Milda's son, my cousin Frankie, had made my life miserable at the end when he was sick and dying. We were always competitive, but now he held the moral high ground. He would haul himself downstairs on his crutches—he was divorced by then and his parents were looking after him—face slightly deformed by the operation and head bald from the chemo. He looked with disgust at the food I'd brought, scalloped potatoes, roast beef and salad. He lowered himself into his chair, grunted, and said, "Carcinogens. That's what all that stuff is."

Like I needed to worry about carcinogens when I lived in a carbon mon-oxide factory.

My aunt made me go out to the Arab place to buy tabboulleh and hummus. The neighbourhood had become mostly Portuguese, but Frankie would not eat a spit-roasted chicken if his life depended on it; by then, his life depended on nothing but time.

They were all like that, the dead and missing relatives—irritating when present, achingly absent when gone, sometimes even irritating when gone. I know I annoyed Aunt Milda even though I was pretty much her only companion until Frankie showed up.

I thought I'd try the direct approach to curing Aunt Milda.

"You know," I said, leaning forward over the kitchen table, "your son really is dead."

"What kind of dead do you call it if I see him around as much as I see you?"

"This happens a lot?"

"Most early mornings. I invite him in, but Frankie won't come. He just sits out on that telephone pole. He won't even talk to me!"

That sounded just like Frankie. When he sulked, he could pull a silent treatment that lasted for weeks.

Then it occurred to me that Aunt Milda was so old, she was seeing the other side already. What did I have to lose by checking the story? I went out to the backyard and walked around my garage home to the alley side.

Nobody takes care of alleys in Toronto, so they're always a mess of trash: a mound of refuse or the sweepings of a street, old kettles, old bottles and a broken can, old iron, old bones, old rags, old memories of the girl I kissed back here on a summer's night after a party in the front of the house. We played hockey here in the fifties, when the only Canadian kids we knew belonged to working class families too poor to move out, the kinds of kids whose parents were orderlies down at the mental hospital at the end of the street. In the long run, hurt by the war, some of our parents made it into that same hospital as patients. Some came out and some didn't.

These Canadian kids of Irish descent were the enemy, the ones you had to out-run in ball hockey, the ones you needed to humiliate before they humiliated you. An immigrant kid never quite gets over having to prove him-self. He keeps looking for the next asshole, and if he looks hard enough, he always finds one.

I climbed up onto my garage roof where I could get a good view of the telephone pole Aunt Milda was talking about without standing out in the street and been gawked at.

What did I expect? Nothing, really, and nothing is what I saw unless you count a bend in the light, a distortion by the crossbar at the transformer. I could have looked longer, I suppose, but I was embarrassed enough already. I climbed down the ladder.

I went back inside to find Aunt Milda looking out the back window, the way I had come. She seemed pale, unhealthy. She needed something.

"You don't drink coffee any more?" I asked.

"It makes me jittery without waking me up."

"Does camomile do anything for you?"

"No. It's like *ersatz*, the stuff we drank during the war, not much better than hot water."

I thought for a while. "Do you remember Tangy Wishniaks?" I asked.

"What are you talking about?"

There was that note of irritation, a special kind of love we demonstrate to those who were once close to us.

"You know, Tangy Wishniaks, a drink they served at the Lakeview Lunch, over at Ossington and Dundas. When I was a kid you or my parents would go there sometimes after mass on Sundays. I always ordered a Tangy Wishniak because the name sounded so weird."

"That's nice."

"Aunt Milda, they're more than nice, they're fantastic! One of those would pick me up for the rest of the boring Sunday afternoon. My father once drank a Tangy Wishniak and it cured his hangover. If that's not a miracle, I don't know what is."

"You were very young when your father died."

"I remember it as if it was yesterday. Listen, I'm going to go out to the Lakeview and get you a Tangy Wishniak."

"I'm not that thirsty. I just had some tea."

"You'll be thirsty by the time I get back."

"What's the big deal with a soda fountain drink?"

"That's just it. This is the last *real* soda fountain drink in the world. Nobody makes those anymore. It will pick you up. You'll see more clearly. It's refreshing the way Coke was supposed to be refreshing but never was."

"Sure," she said, patting the table next to my hand, "get me a Tangy Wishniak, but take your time. I'm going to take a nap."

I didn't want to lie to her, but she might balk if I told her what my real destination was. The Tangy Wishniak was a red herring.

I thought I'd go down to the Lithuanian parish on Gore Vale at Dundas, the one we used to go to when I was a kid. I'd get Father Pete to drop by. He could help out whether or not Frankie was a ghost: on the one hand, the old priest might be able to act like a lay psychiatrist and counsel her; on the other hand, if there was any truth to the ghostly business, maybe he could do an exorcism and take the ghost away. One thing for sure: a Catholic priest was way cheaper than a psychiatrist. Most Lithuanians have peasant roots— they try the cheapest solution first.

I liked to stick to my back alley, so I hadn't been up Dovercourt in a long time. I became uneasy at Dundas Street, feeling not exactly agoraphobia, but a sense of displacement. Let's face it, a man who resides in a heated garage is not exactly a man about town.

The street had a lot of new stores on it. It was amazing how fast the place changed. Dundas around Dovercourt was a neighbourhood that never had a heyday. It was made of slapped-together two- and three-storey red brick storefronts, lively but gritty, boomtown rich in good decades, just plain gritty in the bad ones.

On the southeast corner of Dundas and Ossington, there'd been the Lithuanian Community Centre, a dump of a long, narrow building where the old-time boozers sat around all day, drinking beer. Just south on Ossington had been the Aster Theatre, a cinema or maybe an old vaudeville house from before my time.

Both were gone. In their place stood a Canadian Imperial Bank of Commerce, a long, ugly, stucco building like some kind of elongated, grey lizard that had settled on the south side of the street.

Luckily, the old Lakeview Lunch was still across the way. This was the restaurant where I'd had my first Tangy Wishniak. It was something like black cherry soda, but homemade. I loved the name, one that sang of Slavic aspirations, and every time there was a new waitress, I'd ask her where the name came from.

I'd get this look, like, *what am I, a historian? an anthropologist? a know-it-all?*

Who knew where drink names came from? One of my pals said Jews made the drink and another said it came from Poland. Once, when my father sent me down to the Jewish market to buy some bagels, I'd asked the baker there.

"Hey Jew," I said, "What's a Wishniak?"

He looked at me like I was a child anti-Semite.

Closer to home, we had a butcher who sold Polish sausage. I thought, if he sells Polish sausage, maybe he knows about Polish drinks too.

"Hey Pollack," I said. "What's a Wishniak?"

"Hey stupid kid," he said. "Learn some manners."

We were all less sensitive back then. We insulted one another democratically, competitively. Whoever did it the best, won. Now the rules were different. Nobody was playing rough any more; nobody was playing at all. I guess it was easy for me to say. Hardly anyone knew what Lithuanians were, and those few who did weren't all that warm to us.

The Lakeview Lunch was pretty much as I'd always remembered it: dark wood panelling and booth seating that had always made me feel grown up. But the place was not full of regular people, the way it used to be: local bachelors or store owners who took their meals there and the slightly higher-end drunks who didn't want to drink in the Lithuanian Community Centre across the street.

The place had been discovered by Gen X and Y moms. The everyday food of the past had become the comfort food of the present. Hipsters slipped in here sometimes for meatloaf or a hot chicken sandwich, but they did it ironically.

I took a seat on a stool at the empty counter. I must have flagged the waitress three times, but she still ignored me. At the best of times, I was practically invisible to everyone except Aunt Milda.

Finally, a geezer busboy came banging out of the swinging doors from the kitchen. The waitress didn't notice him either. She practically walked straight through him. He was lean and bony in the way of men who can't afford to retire, and he wore one of those old-fashioned soda fountain hats over a brush cut. He unloaded a stack of milkshake glasses and looked me over.

"You want something?" he barked.

"I'm trying to get a Tangy Wishniak to go."

"A what?"

"A Tangy Wishniak. It used to be on the menu here when I was a kid."

"Man, that's been off the menu for a long time."

"Off the menu?"

"Right, along with malted milkshakes, butter-fried danishes, lime rickeys, mixed grill, flavoured straws..."

"Okay, Okay. I get your point. But is there anyone here who still knows how to make one?"

The geezer pushed his cap forward as he scratched the back of his head.

"Not much to it, really. Soda water, cherry syrup and some kind of so-called secret ingredient. There might be something on the back shelf. I'll take a look."

The double swinging doors went back and forth for a while as he passed through them to the kitchen, and then they hung still for a long time. A very long time. At no point, I should add, did the young waitress even look at me.

Finally, the geezer came out with a big waxed-paper cup that folded at the top and had a hole for the straw. He slapped the drink down on the counter.

"Great," I said. "How much?"

"Forty-five cents."

"What?"

"You think that's too much? This is the last Tangy Wishniak you're going to see for some time, my friend. I squeezed out the last of the secret syrup from a bottle the old owner left behind. Take it or leave it. I'll drink it myself if you're too cheap."

"Okay, okay."

I put two quarters on the counter and didn't wait for change.

On the sidewalk, I realized I was the victim of my own bad planning. I should have bought the Tangy Wishniak for Aunt Milda on the way back. Now I had to go to the rectory with a takeout cup in my hands.

I walked east along Dundas. Downtown looked pretty in the distance, not exactly the Emerald City, but pretty, a clump of towers in silver, black, bronze and gold, like giants standing on the horizon. There seemed to be more of them than I remembered.

I walked on over to Trinity Bellwoods Park, and had an unsettling moment there. It used to be one of my favourite parks when I was a kid and my parents attended church events. My friends and I would range out into the park valley where the Italian men played bocce and the toughs hung out under the Crawford Street Bridge, smoking unfiltered Exports.

But there was no Crawford Street Bridge any more. I could understand a bridge being torn down, but this was not the case. Half the park, a deep valley that was a bit dangerous after dark, had been filled in with earth and made level. Crawford Street was still there, maybe the bridge was still under the street, but even if that was so, the open space beneath the bridge was gone.

Even the emptiness had disappeared.

I imagined all the greasers down there still, cigarettes on their lips, hair covered in Brylcreem, their hair-combing gestures frozen like those of the people who had fled Pompeii when the hot ash rained down.

The old Lithuanian parish stood on the corner of Gore Vale and Dundas, a fifties modernist church inspired by the A-frames of the day, with a bell tower without a bell and a steeple that echoed the traditional roofs farmers put above icons in the old country. It wasn't a belfry so much the idea of a belfry, not so much a steeple as the idea of a steeple. Since hardly anybody went to church much anymore, we were left with the idea of a church.

The church across the street was called Santa Inés, a Portuguese church, but it had been Italian when I was small. I remembered the little kids standing on the steps for photos for their first communions, the boys in black suits and ties and white armbands, a bunch of budding Dean Martins, the little girls in white dresses and bouquets of flowers in their hands, little Shirley Temples, all in a row.

The Portuguese were moving out of the neighbourhood now, the surest sign of that being the place's designation as "Little Portugal" on the street signs. You only get a designation like that after you're dead—it's a grave marker.

I felt like looking inside the Lithuanian church to see if the gigantic wooden Christ was still behind the altar, but the doors were locked. I banged on them a few times just in case the cleaners were working in there, but the church rang hollow. I went down off the steps and around to the rectory on Dundas.

There were two doorbell buttons on the frame, one for the Korean Catholic Church and the other blank. Father Pete must be sharing the church with the Koreans now. He was such a good steward of money that he probably had them on timeshare.

I was going to press the blank doorbell, but I looked at the Tangy Wishniak in my hand.

The waxed paper cup was sweating. I was seized with a powerful thirst and I sat down on the steps. How bad would it be to take just a tiny sip? After all, Aunt Milda was an old lady. The odds were that she wouldn't drink the whole thing anyway.

As I was studying the Tangy Wishniak, the door opened behind me and somebody stepped out. The Korean priest walked down the steps to the sidewalk and headed east without saying anything at all to me.

Without thinking twice, I put my lips on the straw and sucked up a bit of the last Tangy Wishniak on earth.

Talk about refreshing. The whole street became sharper, the way it looks when you walk out of the optometrist's for the first time with a new pair of glasses and realize your eyes have been blurry for the longest time.

I took another sip, and there were the Italian kids across the street on the steps of Santa Inés, standing patiently in the June heat as the photographer squared them up for the group photo. On my side of the road, men stood around in fedoras and raincoats, most of them smoking. I saw a man who looked like my father, or the way I remembered him. He'd been gone a long time.

I took another sip.

A St. Patrick's Day parade was coming along the street from downtown, with parish banners held up on flagpoles and an amateur brass band playing "O Come, O Come Emmanuel," the hymn we learned to sing for whenever our choir visited English-speaking parishes. I could practically sing along the words I had forgotten I still knew:

O come, thou Wisdom from on high,
who orderest all things mightily;
to us the path of knowledge show,
and teach us in her ways to go.

Not exactly Shakespeare, but to the point in a crude way.

This was a lot for an agoraphobic like me to take in one day. Behind the Irish parade I could vaguely see others, people dressed in odd clothes, some of them with feathers. They were a ways off, but I had no desire to study them too closely.

I went whipping back to my place. I moved as fast as I could and still not spill the half cup of Aunt Milda's Tangy Wishniak. I cut through the lane and went straight to my garage, intending to catch my breath before I went into the house.

But when I closed the door behind me, I found Aunt Milda there, sitting on a stool. My cot was gone and so was the stinky kerosene heater that used to make my head swim on cold nights when I cranked it up high. And she wasn't alone. She had a priest with her, a modern priest, a Franciscan in his brown robes, but with a goatee and a small ponytail held together by an elastic band—he looked like a Gen Y priest, a concoction I'd never imagined before. Like everyone else that day, the priest ignored me.

"What's this all about?" I asked. "Who is this priest?"

"This is Father John."

"I was just out looking for Father Pete."

"He's been dead for thirty years."

Right. I knew that. I must have been a little stressed. I sat down on another stool beside her. The Franciscan stayed on his feet, looking straight through me.

"I brought you the Tangy Wishniak," I said.

"What's he saying?" the priest asked.

"He's talking about a soda fountain drink."

"Don't accept anything from him."

"What do you think I am, some maniac? This is my aunt," I said.

The priest started to mutter a prayer and the old Catholic magic began to work. Boredom. I immediately felt like taking a nap.

"Now talk to him," said the priest.

"Dear nephew," she said, as if she didn't know my name, "I want you to listen to me. I'm very old, too old to live in this house. I need to go to a retirement home, so you can't have this place any longer."

"You're not all that old."

"I am."

"Take a sip of this drink. You'll see. It'll pick you up."

"I'm sure it's a very delicious drink, but no thank you."

"What about Frankie? Are you going to move out and leave your son on the telephone pole?"

"Frankie is leaving. Maybe you should go together."

These were the words that I had been fearing.

"You're being very hard on me, Aunt Milda," I said.

"This is what's best."

"What should I do with the Tangy Wishniak? I went to a lot of trouble to get it."

"You drink it."

I was not going to do any such thing. I was going to throw it across the room. I was going to jump up from the stool and make a scene.

But I didn't either of those things. I took a sip of the drink.

It tasted good, a taste from my childhood, one part flavour and three parts memory.

I took another sip, and then another.

I felt light as dust, a speck floating in the air. The currents of wind would carry me far away from this place; I suppose it was about time. But eventually, I would settle somewhere. I would become part of a layer of earth and then, as time passed, a stratum of shale formed by the people of my time: the greasers, the mothers in housedresses, the fathers in fedoras, the street hockey boys, the shopkeepers who had run the stores along Dundas between Dovercourt and Gore Vale, the old boozers who drank away their days at the Lithuanian Community Centre, talking of the homes they had left decades before.

And maybe someday, an archeologist would find us all, like trilobites in shale. When the archeologist chipped away at one layer of shale, my era would come up, and along with it, the smell of our dreams, and the taste of a Tangy Wishniak.

Ming Mei's Year
Sandra Tam

SPRING

At the beginning of spring, our family visits the cemetery.

"*Qing Ming* is the time when Chinese families pay their respects to the ancestors in the spirit world," Mama explains.

When we arrive at the graveyard, my cousin Calvin and I dash ahead of the grown-ups. We trample across the cushiony grass field toward our grandfather's grave. Lao Lao, my grandmother, calls out in Mandarin, "Ming Mei, put on your sweater." She holds out my sweater. It flaps like a flag on a pole.

The wind is strong; it whistles loudly, as though it has something to say.

The daffodils that we planted around grandfather's tombstone last year are now in full bloom.

"Yellow was Lao Ye's favourite colour," Uncle tells me and Calvin. "He said it reminded him of sunshine and happiness."

Mama sweeps dirt away from the tombstone. Lao Lao clears away some leaves and twigs. Uncle lays out food. Calvin reaches for a shrimp dumpling, but Uncle shoos his hand away. The *dian xin* is for Lao Ye in the spirit world.

We lay out a roast chicken and *cha shao*. Pieces of poppy-red barbeque pork glisten in the sunlight. The meaty barbeque smell wafts through the air. I am sure that grandfather can taste the sweet and salty tidbits. We lay out several pairs of chopsticks and a few plastic forks for grandfather and the ancestors.

Uncle tries to light the longevity candles and incense sticks, but the wind blows out the flame. He strikes the match again and again and again before he finally lights the candles. The flames flicker as Uncle arranges the lit up rods by the tombstone. Smoke squiggles from the top of the incense before disappearing into the air.

Mama holds a wad of gold paper to the candle.

"We have to burn money so that Lao Ye can spend it in the spirit world," she explains. Calvin's eyes grow big; he looks confused.

"Don't worry," I whisper. "The money's not real; it's special paper money." We watch the paper shrivel into a pile of black ashes. It smells like sandalwood and camping.

"What will Lao Ye buy?" I ask.

"I think he'll buy a car," says Lao Lao. "Your grandfather loved those old-fashioned Cadillacs with the tail fins from the 1950s."

"I wanna drive!" says Calvin. He steers his pretend car and says, "VROOM! VROOM! Beep! Beep!"

"Your grandfather would definitely buy a house," says Mama. "In his house, he would have a warm fireplace and comfortable furniture. He would hang Chinese paintings and calligraphy scrolls."

"When your Lao Ye was alive, he bought Chinese keepsakes like jade carvings and ceramics that reminded us of our homeland while we settled in this new country. Such meaningful things turn a house into a home," Lao Lao explains.

Mama tells us to bow three times to pay our respects. One, two, three. We watch the candles melt. A robin flies by. She sings her cheerful song of spring. We hear tree leaves rustle softly nearby.

A squirrel scurries by, probably looking for nuts or acorns or things that squirrels like to eat. When he does not find anything, he runs off, snaking around the tombstones. Calvin chases after the squirrel and I chase after Calvin. We run around and around and around until we have no breath left.

The grown-ups pack the food away. We will eat when we get home.

The wind is gusting and howling when we arrive home. From my bedroom window, I watch the clouds spill across the sky. The breeze whips my hair around and brushes my face. I think about how the wind carries the memories of my grandfather, all the way home.

SUMMER

"My mama says summer is the best season," my friend Harriet declares while we skip rope in her backyard.

In between skips, I ask, "What (skip)—makes (skip)—SUMMER (skip)—best (skip)?"

"Maybe skipping makes summer best," replies Harriet. She jumps in. We yell, "Ready! (skip)—set! (skip)—Red (skip)—hot (skip)—PEPPER (skip)!" I spin the rope faster and faster. Jumping red hot pepper makes us hot and thirsty.

Harriet's kitchen smells like coconuts and curry. We sit in front of the fan so it blows our sweaty faces. Harriet's mother serves us tall glasses of pineapple orange juice and mango slices.

"Ming Mei wants to know what makes summer best." Harriet asks her mother after gulping down her juice.

"Sugar-sweet mangoes make summer best," replies Harriet's mother.

"Put sunscreen on before you go outside," Harriet's mother reminds us. She squirts a blob of lotion on our waiting palms. Harriet rubs the white cream into her cheeks until it disappears into her dark night skin.

Maybe sunshine makes summer best, I think.

Harriet and I go to my house to help my grandmother, Lao Lao, in the garden. We pick snow peas from tangled vines. We play hide and seek with the tomatoes; they hide, we seek. We pick the cherry red ones. Lao Lao grows bubblegum pink peonies with a sweet perfume smell.

"When the peony is in bloom, it is more precious than a handful of money," says Lao Lao in Mandarin.

"Maybe gardens make summer best," says Harriet.

After lunch, Harriet's older sister Tasha takes us swimming. Harriet and I swim in the shallow end. Then, we glide down the curly slide and land in the water with a great, big, gigantic SPLASH!

"Maybe swimming makes summer best," says Harriet.

Harriet's mother invites Lao Lao and me for a picnic dinner with their family in the park. We all eat barbeque jerk chicken and spare ribs with guava sauce. Lao Lao brings pyramid-shaped *zongzi*. She shows us how to unwrap the bamboo leaves to eat the glutinous rice dumplings. For dessert, we have key lime pie.

"Maybe picnics make summer best," says Harriet.

That evening, Harriet and I camp out in her backyard. We lie on our backs with our heads outside the tent. Crickets chirp; a dog barks. We sing "Twinkle, twinkle, little star…"

As my eyelids start to get heavy, I ask Harriet, "Do you know what makes summer best?"

"Sleeping outside?"

"Maybe."

"Counting stars?"

"Maybe."

"I give up, what makes summer best?"

"Being friends makes summer best."

FALL

It is fall, and Mr. Boyd is taking our grade two class on a trip to the apple orchard. My classmates and I are so excited that we can hardly sit still. We can't wait to pick bushels of apples straight from the tree.

All of the boys and girls from grade two scramble onto the yellow school bus. Ms. Russo drives the bus down Spadina Avenue, past the tall buildings, over the bridge and onto the highway. The highway turns into a country road, and soon our grade two class arrives at the apple orchard.

"I bet there are a million apples on those trees!" I exclaim. The apple trees stand in straight rows, the branches heavy with fruit.

"Pick as many apples as you like," instructs Mr. Boyd. "But be sure to leave some for others."

"I'm going to pick the biggest apples," I say.

"I'm going to pick the reddest apples," says Sumita.

"I'm going to pick some of each—red, yellow and green apples," says Harriet.

"I'm going to pick the sweetest apples," says Jimmy.

"How do you know which ones are sweetest?" I ask.

"I just do," says Jimmy.

"You sure picked a lot of apples," says Mr. Boyd to me and my classmates from grade two.

"I picked spies and empires," I reply.

"I picked red and golden delicious," says Jimmy.

"I picked McIntosh," says Sumita.

"I picked them all," says Harriet.

"You'll need a big appetite to eat all these apples!" Mr. Boyd says as he counts the overflowing bushels.

"How big?" we ask.

"This big," answers Mr. Boyd with his arms spread way out.

My classmates and I bring apples to school every day that week, and every day the next week and every day the week after that. For three whole weeks, we eat apples: crispy sweet ones and juicy tart ones. We eat apples in the morning, at lunchtime and in the afternoon. Every day, one or more apples a day; day, after day, after day. Soon, my classmates and I get tired of apples.

"Mr. Boyd, there are too many apples," I tell my teacher.

"I'm afraid we can't eat them all," admits Sumita.

"What shall we do with all these apples?" Mr. Boyd asks all of the boys and girls from grade two.

"We could throw them away," says Jimmy.

"My mama says we shouldn't waste food," says Harriet.

"We could save them for winter," suggests Sumita.

"They may go rotten," says Mr. Boyd.

"I could give some to my babysitter," offers Jimmy.

"My grandmother says sharing is a good idea," I say.

"We could give apples to our family and friends," says Harriet.

"Yes, of course!" we all shout.

"Then, we can have a big apple party," says Sumita.

"What a fabulous idea!" everyone agrees.

After school, Mr. Boyd, my classmates and I give apples to our family, friends and neighbours. I take apples to Ms. Lee, the storekeeper in Chinatown. I leave apples for my mother to share with the nurses and doctors at the hospital where she works. Jimmy gives apples to Tasha, his babysitter, who already got some from her sister Harriet. Harriet gives apples to Ms. Russo, who shares them with her young nephew, Ming Mei's cousin Calvin. Sumita gives apples to Ms. Jones, her piano teacher. Mr. Boyd gives apples to all his friends from his running club.

Then, everyone comes to Apple-Fest.

All the neighbours cook specialty dishes for Apple-Fest. Someone brings caramel apples; someone else brews hot apple rum cider. There are apple pies, apple pancakes, apple chutney, apple risotto, apple strudel, apple salads, apple bread pudding and even grilled apple sandwiches.

Everyone eats and sings and dances and plays. Old friends are remembered and new friends are made. Mr. Boyd, my classmates and I declare Apple-Fest a grand success.

"Good thing we picked a million apples straight from the tree," says Sumita.

I pat my full stomach and say, "Next year, we should pick pumpkins."

WINTER

"Brrr! I do not care for the cold, wind and dampness," says Lao Lao in Mandarin.

My grandmother does not like winter. I tug on my boots and pull on my hat. Lao Lao slips on her *mian yi*. She wears her old-fashioned, quilted jacket with the fancy frog buttons all through winter.

Lao Lao and I walk to school. Her glove holds my mitten. We meet my friend Sumita and her mother, Ms. Choudhury, along the way.

"Is Beijing cold in winter?" Ms. Choudhury asks Lao Lao in Hindi.

"Is Beijing cold in winter?" Sumita translates to me in English.

"Is Beijing cold in winter?" I translate to Lao Lao in Mandarin.

"*Dui!*" Lao Lao nods her head, and Ms. Choudhury smiles. When we talk, smoky clouds puff out of our mouths like chimneys.

In the schoolyard, Lao Lao says, "Ming Mei, remember to listen to your teacher." Yesterday, she said, "Remember to share your crayons." Lao Lao's words sound stern, but her eyes are warm like Ovaltine. Lao Lao always reminds me to work hard. I learn all the messages by heart because she says them twice, sometimes three times each.

The next day, I get ready for school but I cannot find my mittens. Lao Lao looks everywhere—in the closet, behind the sofa cushions and under the welcome mat.

"*Aiya!*" Lao Lao shakes her head. "I forget your mother washed them last night." Lao Lao gives me her gloves. In the schoolyard, Lao Lao forgets to tell me to be good. She just heads home with her hands in her pockets. I want to cry out, "You forgot something!" But my tongue feels frozen.

"Why are you wearing grown-up gloves?" asks Jimmy. "Why doesn't your grandmother have a proper winter coat?"

I look away and pretend not to hear him.

"Why doesn't she speak English?"

A chill sweeps over my heart.

Later, I arrive home for lunch, but something is wrong. Why doesn't Lao Lao greet me at the door? I rush into the kitchen. It's smoky; something is burning. Mama is in the kitchen scrubbing the wok in the sink.

"What happened?" I ask Mama. I stand still like a statue, waiting for her answer.

"Lao Lao had some trouble with the fried rice," my mother replies. "Ms. Choudhury will take you to school this afternoon because I have to go back to work."

"Don't worry, Ming Mei," says Lao Lao. "Today the sidewalks are too icy for an old woman to walk."

Sumita, her mother and I walk briskly to school. We shuffle over the slippery patches. The wind feels frosty even though I wrapped my scarf around my neck twice. When we get to the schoolyard, Ms. Choudhury says something to me in Hindi.

"Sometimes when people get older, they forget things," Sumita translates her mother's message to me. "Maybe you can help your *nanni* remember."

Ms. Choudhury's eyes are warm, like Lao Lao's, but not the same. Lao Lao has Ovaltine eyes; Ms. Choudhury has milky *chai* ones. I think about helping Lao Lao, and I feel a little fire light up my insides.

When I come home from school, I put my mittens in my pockets before I hang my jacket on the coat rack. Lao Lao pours me a cup of jasmine tea.

"Drink your tea while it's hot," Lao Lao instructs me.

The next day, I get ready for school. Lao Lao asks, "Where are your mittens?"

"Here they are!" I reply, taking them out of my jacket pocket.

"*Wah!* What a sensible girl you are!" Lao Lao wraps my scarf around my neck twice.

On Saturday, the sun shines bright, and the ice has melted. Lao Lao and I go shopping in Chinatown. We buy bok choy, lotus root and shiitake mushrooms from the fruit and vegetable stall. We buy dried leaves and bark from Ms. Lee's herb store to make soups that give energy and protection from the blustery cold. As we make our purchases, I check off each item from our shopping list so that we don't forgot anything.

Mama makes shrimp wontons in steaming noodle soup for lunch and serves us jasmine tea.

"Drink your tea while it's hot," Mama instructs Lao Lao.

"Brrr! I do not care for the cold, wind and dampness," says Lao Lao, sipping her tea.

"Winter's not so bad," I say, slurping my noodles, "especially when it's warm inside."

Poems
Ken Babstock

25

COMMISSIONERS AVENUE,
ANALYSIS IS THE POORER HALF OF UNKNOWING

And he, Larry, could see for a moment Molly's Diner where he'd eaten the last time they'd turned him out of 54 Division with his jacket and wallet on its rigged up chain and no laces in his runners so he'd had to curl his toes into bird's claws to keep his shoes from dropping off his feet as he walked while holding the left side of his body gingerly, a little impacted at the waist, so breathing had been a little easier if he kept to shallow breaths and looked up out of one eye to see which way was Molly's. He'd ordered a western and removed the peppers with the tines of a fork as the sandwich cooled. A coffee and refill watching the big-faced clock nearing 11 am but not looking to either side as he'd felt others shifting their plates of pie further down the Formica runway. The sun had come in through Molly's big plate window and warmed him where he sat but eating was hard as it laboured his breathing and he was sure, by the western's mottled second triangle, that his ribs had been bruised maybe cracked but whatever.

That was an ok thing to think at the moment because now was bad. Now they'd passed 54 and Molly's and Cherry Street and he knew the docks were off to his left but there were two in back with him and they'd pulled his hat down over his eyes and his jacket up over his head like in a hockey fight just as the cruiser lefted onto Cherry back there. It was dark. One was talking away to the two in front about their last shift and the wife of one of them being no good at curling and how Cheryl's brother Jack was giving him a hard time about widening his driveway without the city's permission and one in front got happy about having been given tickets to a game this coming Wednesday and he exhorting the others to come for pops afterward and he'd give them the play-by-play. The other one—the one sitting to his left, and leaning in and holding the thumb of his, Larry's, left hand back against its own wrist making his arm bent and wing-like and shoot pain up through the elbow into his neck and shoulder—was whispering some pretty menacing shit into Larry's ear about being worthless dreck and knocking a clue into his shitass brains with a tire iron after he'd broke both his ankles and cut off his alky-soaked tongue. Larry pressed his knees together.

And kept his head lowered. It'd be best if he did nothing to piss off the other three who were into the price of land in Muskoka as compared to places south on Lake Erie where there were bikers besides it would only get more polluted with options for landfill dwindling and no end in sight for steelworks around Hamilton. The window was open slightly and a breeze entered the car. Larry heard the tires on gravel now and was picturing in his mind's eye the taller poplars on the Leslie Spit and the low stands of reddish dogwood and some other brambly plant he didn't know the name of but under which tunnels and a kind of system of catacombs, not elaborate but enough to provide wind-guard, had been set in by years of use by people Larry knew and many he'd never spoken to but had shared something with standing over a can fire and laughing through his teeth. He could see also the weirdly bent metal rebar that stuck out of the shelves of concrete piled up around the water's edge and how it looked alien or maybe like entombed or calcified entrails of animals long dead and the lake would get up some nights and wash in under the slabs making slapping and growly noises you could listen to for hours if you had something in you that night. The car stopped and he heard a door from a second car open and swing shut again just feet from them. The one with his thumb said get out, fuck, and put a hand at the back of his head and bent him over like they were entering a squad car not exiting 'cause it was wrong to have one nevermind two of them in the back with him he knew. A beer can opened with a click and hiss and he wished he could have just a hit of it but just then one of them kicked his right foot hard from behind and he could feel himself going over fast and his shoe flying off as he went back and then the hard ground that knocked the wind out of him as he was trying to say Get me to the cell you shits and then it started in earnest the blows and kicks and they picked him up again and held him aloft and the blood he could taste thick in his mouth which wasn't that bad but he wanted to see them if it was going to be this way tonight but his eyes were quickly swelling shut like parts of a chicken and filling with blood also 'cause it ran down from his head in syrupy rivers damming and backing up for a while at his brows but then pouring in. Head injuries, Larry knew, bled like snot and their reverberations shuddered back into the past and out well into the future whatever that was now.

SOVEREIGN

Hospital lobby staging a jumble sale, so being discharged's
    like viewing San Marco. The Habs in deep
down in Philly, Michael Ballack has sent Liverpool
    home. Light of midday like chlorine after

the postnatal dim, those Danby mums on hardboard dulled
    down the ward. His Baba and Dedo took him
home in the Honda. Hollowed out. Air strains clean through;
    I'm a canoe. Ghost-nippled, rose-petalled,

cross-eyed narcoleptic—no power higher than myself save
    what I ceded to the State at birth. Sweet William!
Not my son, blooms trimming the parking garage, bruised
    strip of the vast conurbation, they nice up

the joint, along with the mayor. Aced the Apgar. Not
    an improper moment, is it, to think the city
might as yet work, bear out *Solvitur Ambulando* at street
    level while no one's looking. That journalist,

held in Gaza in a locked room, incredulous at travellers'
    impatience the day he's released, six
short weeks later stood carping at the absence of buses
    in London. Pillow cloud, cinnamon roll,

health card, I feel…*altered.* We change, and change back
    as though adaptation were Cuba. Walking
traffic down the sunless canyon of Grenville; shouldn't
    one open their face to me, here? Am I not

the sun, lugging these birthing bags and cut flowers and
    charged with keeping a lid on explosions
into futurity into what's next when will the bricks speak
    passing the raised gate of the pay-parking

an Escalade pulls out and the banded arm drops, candy
    cane guillotine, to clean the overheated mind.
Knocked out. Knocked into the engine oil and cellophane.
    Knocked back toward *techne,* to-do lists,

today's handlot of small majesties with mass, surface, scent.

THE DON WHERE IT EMPTIES

King subsumed by Queen, a single monarch's processional
under metal banners slows crossing the bridge—
the pigeons, like Riopelle, are putting the paint on thick
and human volunteers walk mastiffs, pit bulls,
diabetic shepherds past high end
furniture, excavated sink holes,
and new "green" condos.
Wildlife, like phalangists, blend
with commuters and the minor league coaches;
Crows of Tokyo, Elephants of Kenya, Coyotes of Burnaby,
the Creeping Southern Possums of Pickering literally freezing
their tails off in hopes of passing as rats. Here at the railing
we're public art, watching the stew thicken. Time was
a river was reliable as a standard metaphor for Time—Eastern
Standard. Once upon a fork tine
a carp called out into the mouth it fed.
The mouth empties a FedEx brown
into lake-liner slips sleeping away the exodus
of even the idea of making anything worth exporting.
What if I stood on the step and declared my love
for everyone?

Cough and Brume

Rawi Hage

My son is late. A few nurses have passed by my room since he called this morning, and a little while ago a shady white apron holding a folder and a pen stood still as I opened my eyes: another one of those modern healers, levitating at the edge of my sheet, checking off boxes on a piece of paper, assessing charts and tonsils before sending me back home.

The man in the next bed is fond of football games and bells. He is dying and he has to remind everyone of it until the end—until his palms give up, his eyeballs roll into his head and disappear, and his church calls for prayers. A million and one cigarettes are hosted in his chest, and his coughs release smog and eject curses. If it weren't for the divide between our beds, his spit and a brume of toxic fumes would have reached over and killed me by now.

Now I see two vignettes moving to his side, one black and one white. I mistrust doctors and I will refuse the presence of a priest on my deathbed. I told that to my son the other day, and he said: It won't be for a long time, for a long time, Dad.

My son's God-fearing wife pretended she didn't hear me. She is afraid that the Prince of Darkness or some saint with a funny haircut will come and take her away for associating with me. But I have always hated the swinging incense and the smoke and those horrific chants of the clergy that come with a special tariff for the gullible and the poor. Yes, yes, on many occasions I handed the priests money before and after the funerals of relatives and friends who raced me to the finish line and won. During the war years, I stepped behind sacred altars and pulled out a few bills and buried them in those priests' garments, in tunnel pockets layered with mysteries, hypocrisies and archaeologies of oppression and deceit. I did it because the dead asked me to, because I am a proud man and a good friend, because something has to be done or said before you cover cadavers in soil and swing shovels. But in my youth, I refused to kneel and kiss the priest's ring. I knew what those fingers were capable of, fingers with the sharp cut of diamond rings and a long, wicked reach.

I am a rational man, a man who has never knelt, and I pride myself that I have cared about lives and not eternal souls. Many years ago, I was a young man living in that garden city, Beirut—yes, it was once a city filled with gardens and red roofs and clear water, and wells, many wells. I pride myself on knowing history, and especially the history of my land. I could remember the exact euphony of the name Beirut, if only this dying man would stop coughing…Yes, the word *Beirut* comes from the ancient word *Birûta*, which refers to a well in Semitic languages (and I don't mean just Hebrew). It is *burtu* in Akkadien, *be'er* in Hebrew, and something very similar in Phoenician, and *bîr* in Arabic. After Alexander ravaged our shores, the Greeks turned it into *Bérytos*, and the Romans then turned it into *Berytus*, and the Arabs later on, *Bayrût*. And much later on, those silly American soldiers pronounced it *Bay Ruth*!

Anyway, not to be too pedantic, but like to I keep reminding myself that I am a rational man. Once, as a young man, I heard that a friend of mine was sick. He was a dear friend, and later on in life we travelled together all over Europe. This time when I was a young man, I went to pay my friend a visit. I walked down the narrow streets. I saw my friend's mother in a panic, rushing the stairs, followed by two despicable women who loved to spy and gossip. I followed the women and I saw my dear friend, Kourban, in a sweat. He was delusional. He was turning his head left and right, the sweat dripping like nectar on his face and down his collar. He didn't recognize me when I tried to talk to him. The two women prepared incense and herbs, and then they burned the herbs and muttered superstitious hymns, something about walnuts trees and spirits. They passed a smoky tray to each other above my friend's head. I looked at Kourban and I thought: he is gone.

I rushed to find Dr. Touhmeh. What a brilliant, enlightened man he was, that doctor. He had studied with the French, and then he became a doctor and later fought with the French in Algeria against the Germans during the war. I told him what I'd seen and the fever I had felt on my friend's forehead. He cursed the women. He said they should be arrested and put in jail for witchcraft. He asked me to run to the icemaker Abou-George and tell him to hurry to Kourban's house with two large blocks of ice. In those days, when Beirut was old and had red bricks for its roofs and was a garden of a city, there were no fridges. Everyone bought ice in blocks and stored the blocks in an icebox. I ran to Abou-George's home. His wife told me he was at the Zaroub Café down the street, so I rushed to the café, and when I arrived I caught my breath and shouted that the doctor needed ice for my dying friend, and if anyone had seen the icemaker to send him rushing to my friend's house with two large blocks.

The icemaker had just left the café, so a few men stood up and ran after him, and then I had the idea of asking the rest of the men to hurry to their iceboxes at home and pick up what they could, and rush to my friend's house. The wife of the café owner stood in the middle of the street and shouted to all the other women in the neighbourhood, and a few minutes later, I saw women with curved aprons full of ice hurrying toward my friend's house, cold drips wetting their thighs and leaving moist trails on the dusty streets.

I arrived at Kourban's house and saw the doctor pouring water from a bucket on my friend's face. And then, when he saw the women with their heavy aprons, he ordered them to pour all the ice in the tub. No one was stingy back then, even though the women all knew that their food would soon go bad and they would have hungry husbands on their backs, swinging the icebox doors, sitting at kitchen tables grinding their teeth like wolves and bears. No, these women knew that they had to save the life of this man they had known as a child. They shouted and rushed to the tub, and then they kneeled all wet on their knees and started to pray and chant. And the doctor, a rational man whom everyone respected, asked them to stop praying because the coming of saints on chariots of fire might melt the ice and make the water warm. Besides, the doctor added, chants suggest the nearness of death, and that would make the patient and his mother alarmed, and that would bring higher temperatures to their foreheads. And then the doctor (what a doctor he was; I always wanted to see one of my sons become a doctor) asked me to lift my friend by the shoulders while he held him by the knees, and we walked toward the tub and laid my friend down there in cold ice. Because his body was boiling with fever, my friend started to shout and moan, and he called to his mother and told her to keep away from the stove. The women moved toward the bathroom, curious and needing to witness the melting of the ice so as to convince their husbands that fasting can save souls, and that going hungry for one night is worth a man's life, and that God would repay them for their good deed and one day reward their bellies with sweets and soft hands. The doctor told these women that their breath and close faces brought warmth like that of the animals who had surrounded the Holy Child, and that their whispers could melt the glacier and bring on the flood, so they went back to the living room to scoop up their moist aprons and whip them around their sweaty faces, and the aprons that mopped their lips cut their murmurs in half and interrupted their tales of the importance of the cold and the people who come from the cold.

Like I said, I am a rational man. And ironically enough, I stumbled on rationality through my education by priests—those Jesuits, to be precise. In the end, they, I believe, were fond of the Enlightenment, and that is why I always knew they were heretics, to say the least. They arrived with the French army and stayed after the soldiers left. My eyes skimmed through the million and one pages they offered me to read. I read Proust by candlelight, Molière when I was sick (*Le Malade imaginaire* was my favourite piece of theatre), Rousseau when I escaped to the mountains. I tell you, my fingers licked the ink of many imaginary worlds, and these places stayed in my mind like indelible stains. That is why, later on, I decided to take a car and drive through Europe with my friend Kourban.

We cut through Syria, Turkey, Bulgaria, France, and we arrived in Holland, where Kourban met a Dutchwoman three times his height. Her shoulders were strong, her face pale and round. I teased him and made jokes about his wedding night. I imagined him covered with tulips and climbing all the way up so he could reach her breast, or standing with his face at the height of her pubic hair. How convenient, I said, and I laughed. And I remember him laughing too, God save his soul. We are generous people, and Kourban was no exception. He bought the Dutchwoman (whose name I have forgotten now) flowers by the dozen, and every time we visited her house we would show up with food and many gifts. He asked her to marry him. To our surprise, she agreed, but she declined to come back with us to Beirut. And when my friend asked her why, she pulled out an old photograph of sand dunes and camels and shook her head. My friend protested and tried to tell her that our land has no desert, that he'd never seen a camel in his life. Water, he said. And trees! he gestured, his arms high like branches. And jasmine, he said, as he stuck his fingers below his nose and breathed deeply. And mountains and snow! he shouted in French.

The Dutchwoman offered us milk, pea soup and meat, and then we drove back south, taking a detour to the communist countries. We spent like kings. In Sophia we paid the owner of a restaurant a little bit of money, and he invited the local women and a music band and offered food and wine, and we danced all night and ate all night, and it didn't cost us two liras back then. Like I said, we are generous people, so we treated everyone at the restaurant to drinks, and everyone danced that evening. Soon, many people arrived because the owner had invited his family and friends, and we knew that he had done so to increase the bill, but at the end of the evening, no matter what, we paid it. It was nothing. It was the 1960s and Lebanon was at the beginning of its financial peak. The petro-dollars started to crowd our banks because we were the first in that region to emulate the Swiss banks and their policy of secrecy. If only those priests could have seen us spending and dancing. If only they could have imagined the gluttony, the shaking of flesh, and me and Kourban improvising dances in a fusion of styles and folkloric steps.

Those priests had taken me in as an orphan because my father had died from the cold and because my mother washed the priests' white sheets and ironed de Gaulle's soldiers' uniforms. They opened my eyes to what is beyond our narrow street. But what a street it was: dusty, and filled with love and poverty. What a street it was: the jasmine, the long trees. None of that is left now. Our house was in the alley because my father refused to buy the house on the dusty road. He hated the dust that rose from beneath caravans, and he hated the huff of the horses. Ah, the decorated chariots that passed beside our street. They were red with ribbons, and as little boys we used to ride on the backs of the chariots until the driver hit us with his whips. My mother would shout from the balcony, telling us not to ride those horses.

My mother—what a mother! She worked hard and raised us well. Madame Zahra, who was married to a French commander, gave all the neighbourhood women, including my mother, jobs at the French barracks. They rode the chariot down to the beach where the French had built their barracks after they and the British and the Australians liberated us from the Germans. My mother washed the soldiers' laundry, mended their uniforms and cleaned their floors. My mother loved the French; she even learned a few words from them. I used to laugh at her mispronunciations when she ordered us around in French, waving a stick or her fist.

And Madame Zahra—maybe her husband was just a French soldier, I can't remember—made sure that the women in the neighbourhood who worked for the soldiers were treated well, and she warned her husband that these women's husbands and sons would not tolerate wandering fingers or any of that French kissing and those romantic jokes. And my mother always com-pared the Frenchmen to those Turks who took her up north to the Anatolia. What a life that woman had, what strength. In her youth she had worked for a prominent Christian feudal family. She cleaned the house and took care of the children. And when the Turks came and sent that family into forced exile, my mother went with them. They travelled on horse and on foot for a month, until they reached Turkey. She became famous when she slapped the Turkish soldier who tried to molest her. She shouted at him and kicked him, which made even his commander laugh. She became famous in her village when the Turks were defeated, and the Christian family and my mother were liberated.

But no one had told the Australians about the rules when it came to our women. The Australians were always drunk. They sold everything they owned for a drink. Our neighbour Souad made a fortune buying their quilts, and even their shoes, for nothing. Souad would come back from visiting the Australians with thick English wool blankets and first-class Canadian white flour, and she sold everything to the neighbours, and the blankets turned into dresses and the flour bags turned into men's underwear. You could see our women with soldiers' hats, our men with large vacant shoes, shuffling their feet in the hollows of the boots of the giant Australian soldiers. And our men gave those soldiers cheap arak, and waited until they were drunk and asleep, and stole the wheels off their cars and everything else they could get their hands on. Some of those soldiers drank so much that they got sick and died.

My father also got sick and died, and he left us at the mercy of an uncle who made us, me and my brother, work with wood and nails. I became a carpenter and a reader. In books I found freedom and mighty hammers. I made beds, chairs and tables, and with what little I earned I bought books that I stacked in wooden boxes under my mattress. My father, my mother said, had died from walking in the cold. In my family we feared the cold and the snow. We valued wool, fires and heart-warming tales.

Once, on a Christmas day, my mother gave us a bath in a low, wide metal bucket (my mother always washed us on Christmas). Playfully, I splashed my mother with water and soap, and my mother hit me on my naked thighs. I was nude and wet, and I pushed over the bucket and punched my mother on her shoulder and ran outside of the house, bare as God had created me. It was snowing outside. During those days, that city of gardens and jasmine covered itself in a thin coat of snow in the winter. My mother was so terrified that I would catch a cold and die coughing like my father she ran through the streets after me, screaming her lungs out. I was caught by the warm hands of the baker and brought back into my mother's arms, and she rushed me to the fire, wrapped me in a quilt, and called an Arab healer, and the Arab healer came and used on me an old Chinese technique called cupping. He burned little bits of paper in little cups, waited until the cups were warm, and then laid them on my little back. And my skin swelled inside the cups like sand dunes beneath little red suns. Many years later, I tried to do the Arab's trick on my sick wife, but the paper slipped from my hand and I burned my wife's shoulders. I was never a healer or a believer, but I always cared for the lives of others.

As if this sick man next to me hadn't inhaled enough fumes in his life, here is a priest filling the room with dust and incense! Oh, how these gods hold you as an infant and never let you go. They make you recognize their smells through the decaying corpse, the holy water and the wine.

Now I am suffocating and coughing myself. I am going to ring that bell and complain to the nurse or the fire department. Where is my son to rescue me from these masquerades? When I die, I won't mind being reduced to dust, poured in a gold bucket and quietly carried away. I want my ashes sprinkled in that village where my mother took us in the summer on the back of a chariot pulled by a donkey or a mule. Ah, the welcome we had back then, in that village with the mill and the river filled with crescents and little stones. But who am I kidding? That village was swallowed by the big city and turned into cement and hideous stone, and the river has dried, and my cousins sold their houses and left for Australia and Brazil. Some of them even ended up in Cuba. I heard one of them become a high official with Castro—or was it Batista? I'd be surprised if it was Castro because, knowing our kind, we always stick to money and high places.

I thought about finding my cousins once. I thought about taking a plane from Montreal to Cuba in search of their kids or some memory of them, but my son laughed and said, You're better off searching in Miami. Besides, those Latin people always take their mother's surname so you would be looking for a million Gonzales. But I remember those cousins like yesterday. They taught me how to climb fig trees and how to wrestle and fight. Useful— all of it was useful. A taste of blood from the ground makes you a man who respects the harshness of the earth and the value of the land. When the British came to our land after they defeated the Vichy French, they brought large fair-skinned Australians, and those soldiers, under our sun, turned their skin into pink uniforms and their necks into red collars. Victorious, they gave up their guns and used their hands only to hold drinks and fight. They got drunk all the time and sang, and wobbled their way back to their military compounds. Once they molested Zalfa, the mayor's daughter, when she was on her way home. Many of us locals gathered around the mayor's house and swore revenge. We waited for the soldiers at night behind the tavern doors, when they were drunk enough and chanting their war songs on our sidewalks. We prepared the thick buckles on our belts and held our sticks and stones. We attacked the soldiers and made their heads bleed. For centuries our land was treated like a whore so we protected our women. Everyone left with a bruise on their head.

We had a simple life. Our women covered themselves only on their way to the churches and to see their saviour. On Sundays, the bell rang and we dressed up for church. We ate meat once a week and fasted on Friday. We prayed. We danced at weddings and cried at funerals.

I never thought I would be so close to a priest again. And here I am in a foreign land, in a hospital, only a skin of an onion away from those long-robed men. My son should be here soon. Enough! Let them pull these tubes from my arm. I am well. I am very well. I am not dying. I'll pack my few clothes and cross the room and leave behind the brume of the holy man. The TV never ceased until the prayers started. Anyone who loves sports so much ought to die in the open air not in a brume of fog…

If my mother was still alive, she would shout: Respect! Respect, my son, respect! And I would say, It wasn't my fault that you sent me to school. It wasn't my fault that I opened foreign books and saw a glimpse of the other side. I am a man of contradictions, but so is my land. We are a hybrid of cultures and invading religions. But in contradiction there is openness. Well, yes, yes: We Lebs, we were always accused by some of our neighbours of selling out to French colonial forces. The other Arabs mocked us. They mocked our dialect that is infested with French and Italian words. They mocked our lavish ways of living, our snobby ways. I hear them saying: Who do those Lebanese think they are?

But I say: You all flocked to our land. You came in the 1950s, escaping despotic regimes. You were all hosted, tolerated, and you wrote books, hung out in cafés and smoked, and married our women. And yes, we Lebanese brought something to our region. We brought foreign cultures and blended them with the local culture. We brought music and literature. Yes, and what is wrong with bringing in things from the West? So what is wrong with composing the first Arabic song without the sound of a drum? What is wrong with breaking an archaic language open with a new one? We started a movement called Al-Nahda, a new style of literature that broke with the old. Tell me, what is wrong with establishing the first press in our region, what is wrong with having freedom of the press, what is wrong with building the Egyptian film industry? And what culture does not borrow or steal or modify? The West took many things from us Arabs!

I see a woman crying in the hallway. The priest is quiet; even his smoke is settling.

Maybe the fellow next to me has ceased. I hear no cough; the bed doesn't squeak.

I am in the presence of death again. Not that I fear it. I know exactly how it feels to be dead—well, how it doesn't feel. I was one of the very few to survive a horrible car bomb explosion. It happened right next to my store. It was a miracle. Well, here I am being a Christian again. As much as I try to fight the superstition, I can't get rid of language and tradition. Anyway— the bomb exploded and it threw me back a few metres. I was unconscious; I didn't feel a thing. Nothing at all. And afterward I thought, That is what death must be like. Notice I didn't say, *what it feels like*. I said, what it must *be* like. Because to *feel* death—or anything—you need some kind of pulse and, consequently, life.

Here is my daughter-in-law. My son must be parking the car. He is always late.

The man next to me has stopped coughing, and the brume of the priest has settled.

I guess I can leave now.

Poems
Marge Lam

43

CHINATOWN EAST

Keep holding me like this
and help me untie my birth language
my first language
steeped in bruises, knotted up in a child's still body
petrified with fear
words thrown at me
alcoholic bodies raging into me
embedded like ceramic shards
all around my little heart
me, so small and already convinced
my home felt like captivity

When I sought my freedom
learning this new language
all around me
language of the good people
where families kissed and hugged each other
and parents asked their children how they were

I began to beg
for brown bag lunches
embarrassed by my thermoses of fragrant rice
stewed in pork fat
wanting to belong between
pieces of white bread
I ran into the arms of British table manners, fine cheeses
English literature, Led Zeppelin
feeling myself evaporating into creamy skin
bleached hair
steel cold blue eyes
took me many decades to realize
I got lost
trying to disappear

Now, as I begin to relax
in your embrace,
I find myself
a little shy
surprised by my greediness
for your 5,000-year-old
Fujian phrasings
found in the singsong rhythms of
our Taiwanese tongues

So teach me our old language of love
with enough patience
untie all these crunchy knots
and unfurl my native tongue
help me make room to express this want
in between my legs
all through my body of ancestral wounds
drip hot words into my ears
I am ready to come home

THE BEACHES

Would you identify this tree with me
washed up and dishevelled
upturned
roots naked, pointing to the sky

tangled with pebbles, stones, ice and sun

Majestically exposed
as if to say
this is how I could stand tall
you see
all the fine threads I wove
deep into the ground
underneath the skirt of this earth
I am the colour of copper, rubies, fire and heat

Torn from my roots
I have tumbled
with the moon tides
bounced and twisted
with winter storms

And it is here
off this soft shore
I return
to listen to
my last lullaby.

ASHBRIDGE'S BAY PARK

I have been returning to this space
between rocks
a sitting place

the curve of my back
held by ancient minerals

I come to rest
my body weighed down by

concrete tight
internal armour

I relate to this water
beautiful body that brings me peace

one that sparkles in the sun
one that holds the cormorants and seagulls afloat

water I look into
and swear is clear and clean
but I know
has been used as a container

I understand
this allusion of pristine

as pain writes into my cells
unmarked and invisible.

YONGE AND BLOOR

Like a strenuous love affair
this city exhausts me
leaving me worn out, giddy and
spread way too thin
and in a way, underneath
rapid hearts
skipping beats,
I hear
emptiness

Reminding me of those
rush-hour faces
the tightly drawn jaws
stresslines mapping the space
in between brows

we pack ourselves
in urban exhaustion
sluggish
through two intersecting arteries
until we are pumped into
rapid rockets
bloodlines of travel
in this commuting city

Even when we can be still we want to keep running
and when we have one moment
we occupy our lives
until our minutes overlap each other
tenfold
an impossible metabolic rate.

A Pair of Parades
Daniel David Moses

1.

When I phone my mother, Blanche Ruth Jamieson Moses, born in 1924, to wish her a happy birthday, she challenges me.

"So how old am I?"

"You don't look a day over eighty!"

She rarely talks about the past—she's so present—so when she mentioned that, once upon a time, she'd been in the Santa Claus Parade, she got my attention.

The first Santa Claus Parade, such as it was, took place the second day of December 1905. Santa Claus arrived by train at Union Station and was greeted by Mr. and Mrs. Timothy Eaton. Santa then walked through the streets to the Eaton's store.

My own experience of that parade, once upon another time, was always on television and only in black and white. Though my parents might take or send me into the actual city of Toronto in the summer for the CNE or to visit family who lived here, the televised town where that parade took place, sometimes through electronic snow, was always somewhere beyond the horizon. It was not any part of my quotidian imaginings, although at night it was certainly often a distant light.

I remember to ask about The Parade as we drive north on Highway 6, Mom at the wheel, on our way to pick up my sister, Debora. It's the start of our Victoria Day weekend visit.

"What do you want to know about that for?"

"I was just wondering what the city was like back then. You grew up there?"
She checks the rearview mirror. "Grandma and Grandpa," she says,
speaking of her own parents, my grandparents, Minnie Davis and George E.
Jamieson, now both long dead, "Grandma and Grandpa moved to Toronto.
Grandma ran a boarding house over on Bleecker Street, in a row of houses
in the block, I think, north of Carlton, a block east of Sherbourne..."

It was probably in the last year I attended York University, 1976, that my
friend Wendy and I decided we'd make the journey down from Downsview,
at that time a solid ninety-minute commitment on the TTC each way,
to attend The Parade. She was from out of town, Montreal, and knew The
Parade, too, as I did—by reputation—so I guess we both thought it would be
fun. We might finally experience something of childhood we'd missed.

My grandmother Minnie was born in 1904, and my grandfather George E.
Jamieson—there's no clarity in the family now as to whether the never-used
middle name was Elijah or Elias—was born in 1900. So I'm guessing now
that my grandparents were living in the city when my mother was a teenager,
certainly in the late thirties, during the Great Depression. Which may explain
why they'd made the move in the first place and starts to explain how a
Cayuga/Tuscarora Indian girl ended up way back then in—I'm imagining—
a red and round bounce of a dress accompanying Santa's sleigh down
University Avenue.

But 1976 was the year the Eaton's company withdrew its support from the
event—I think old Lady Eaton had finally died—and I remember Wendy and
I were disappointed in the quality of the floats: we were, after all, students
of the Department of Fine Arts. We were also dispirited by all the popcorn,
wrappers and cigarette butts the crowd left behind, by the surly cops herding
the crowd back with steel fences at the corner of University and Queen,
and by the kids cranky in the cold.

"It was a three-storey place," my mother says, "with two rooms on the third
floor, and one large room at the front, and one more other small room on
the second floor, and folks from home would come and stay there when they
first moved into town. Grandma had all kinds of them. She had a lot of single
women from other reserves, too. They'd stay with Grandma for a while
and then get jobs and move out. And sometimes, sometimes," she groaned,
"I had to share my room—and my bed!"

Any last possibility of the hoped-for childhood fun disappeared when Wendy dropped the news of a suicide in our residence at York. It was a boy who shared my first name. Wendy was on the residents' council and had to hurry back to campus for a closed meeting about it—she probably shouldn't have even told me—but I was offended by all the secrecy and wanted to argue about the decision to keep it quiet, "for the family's sake." So we ended our experience of parade day riding the subway north and buses west in silence.

"There was a lane right by our house," my mother remembers, "and it ran behind all the houses in that row. Grandpa had a garage there for his car. He always had a car, always kept it clean and shiny. He was forever polishing that car. It always looked so good."

In the late 1920s, CFRB started broadcasting an entire month of programs following Santa's journey from the North Pole to Toronto. A month of that and everyone was excited for Santa to arrive.

"Uncle Ted," Mom says, turning off the highway into the shopping mall parking lot, "Uncle Ted had a bike that year. Aunt Barb had a job at the drugstore on the corner and she had a bike, probably so she could do deliveries. We went to school just east of there on Winchester Street. Even Cecil Montour, one of the boarders, had a bike. I think he was Delaware. This one time I was late for school and Cecile offered to give me a ride. So I kept bugging Mom and Dad 'til I got a bike too. They saved up for it. It was second hand but it was mine!"

Saint Nicholas, a saint for merchants as well as children, was born on the coast of what today is Turkey, a town called Lycia. Little else is known about his life except he was the Bishop of Myra. Many miracles are credited to him.

"But The Parade? What do you remember about The Parade?"
    She pauses a long pause. "Not much. Not much really. Just all the faces, all the faces looking at me."
    Debora's arrival ends the interrogation.
    A short while later, on the drive home, my mother remembers to mention something. "By the way," she says, "I have to get up early Monday. For The Parade."

2.

So on Victoria Day, known on the Six Nations Reserve as Bread and Cheese Day, my eighty-four-year-old mother is up and out of the house by eight thirty. She and the other Red Hat Ladies have to finish decorating their float by nine thirty in time for the judging.

Our story is that Queen Victoria, in recognition of the Six Nations' service and loyalty to the Crown during her reign, instituted an annual distribution of gifts. Why white bread and cheddar cheese? I've never heard an explanation of this detail. But the annual distribution is the centre of a secular festival. Every year, people come out or come home and gather and, following a parade through the village of Ohsweken, line up outside the Community Hall to receive fresh baked bread, sliced inches thick, and a chunk of tangy orange cheese.

The Red Hat Ladies, my mother reports on her return, won first prize.
"We're not supposed to be making money. This club, it's just for fun."
But with their float decorated with banners, sashes and teddy bears, and all the ladies dressed up in their best hats and overcoats—it was a chilly weekend—and with their umbrellas twirling, all that richness of scarlet, crimson and ruby, with flashes of cherry, mauve, lilac, lavender, wine and plum, the flat-bed truck must have seemed a nearly psychedelic vision of Six Nations womanhood in the rain.

My mother has always favoured red but says she remembers the dress she wore in the Santa Claus Parade as blue, trimmed with white fur. But I prefer to think it was red and that Santa and his parade were the cause of her love for the colour.

"You should have seen the people," Mom says, "all the people. Riding in The Parade like that, you get to see them. All those faces, just going on forever."

Chill, Hush

Jen Sookfong Lee

Maybe the one thing people should know about me is that I hate my house. It sounds mean, doesn't it, like I'm telling everyone that I secretly stick pins into a voodoo doll that looks like my brother, or that I overfed my pet Guinea pig when I was nine just so I could watch it die. The house hasn't done anything to deserve all this ill will. In fact, it just sits there on this ordinary street in East Vancouver, its front covered with red bricks, the lawn lined with a row of rhododendrons. I suppose architects might hate how boxy it is, or how the textured stucco on the sides just collects dirt and bird shit. It's squat and practical and you would never notice it if you were driving by. Really, it's nothing more or less than a respectable house. But I hate it.

It's mostly empty these days, empty air in the long hallway, circling in on itself. Sounds come from the basement, like whispers or sighs, as if the rooms are lonely and have started talking to each other, each word like a breath. I don't go down there much, not since my brother moved out and took all his stuff with him, except for his desk, which still stands under that small, high window. It was only after he left that I found words scratched into the varnish on the top: "I am a mouse."

My mother accumulates almost nothing to fill the rooms or hang on the bare walls. The only thing I remember her buying for the house in the last two years is a crocheted doll whose skirt hides the extra roll of toilet paper in the bathroom. When I came home from school that day, it was sitting proudly in the middle of the coffee table, its wide-brimmed, yellow hat flopping over one brown eye.

"You see," my mother said to me in Chinese, "she looks like you. Same lips."

I turn the key in the lock like I do every morning, hear the satisfactory click that means everything is locked up inside. Sometimes, when the morning is dark and there's a chill hush in the air, I imagine a stream of demons and shrieking lady ghosts following me like an otherworldly parade. I scare myself so much that I never look behind me when I hear a sound; what if I come face to face with a hungry spirit who looks just like me, except with a white face and long, tangled hair and fingers that could pierce my cheek with the slightest touch? I can hear it now, hissing at me, "You can run, Margaret, but I will always be faster than you." I've been going to school for eleven years and I've never forgotten to lock the door once.

I know that my mother watches me walk down the street. She stands in the big living room window and thinks that no one can see her because of the floor-length sheers. Not too many curtains can hide her red cardigan. If it's sunny, the light will reflect off her glasses and shoot two beams of light into the street through the window. I never look behind me, but I know she's there because she always is, the sheers like a fog around her body. I wonder sometimes what she does all day alone in the house like that. By the time I come home, not much has changed; she hasn't painted the kitchen or finished knitting a sweater for my brother or anything. Usually, she's sitting on the couch watching Chinese television and smiles at me when I arrive.

"How was school?" She'll say it like she doesn't really care, like I could say that I sliced open Amanda Gruen's head with a sharpened protractor because she spiked a volleyball into my face during gym, and the expression wouldn't change.

"Fine."

"Are you hungry?"

"No."

"Well then, I'll get you something to eat." And she'll walk off toward the kitchen and make something ridiculous like hand-cut french fries or a full breakfast with bacon and hash browns. I've been to other people's houses, and their moms make snacks like peanut butter and banana sandwiches, or crackers and cheese, easy things like that. But not my mother. Yesterday, she had six Scotch eggs ready by the time I changed my clothes.

Other people worry about time. My mother fills as much of it as she can with meat and rice and the steam that billows up from an uncovered pot. Every dish is like a collision of salty and sweet, hot and sour, crunchy and gooey.

Before I was born, my parents owned a diner and my mom did all the cooking while my father took the orders, mostly because my mother doesn't speak English. But that was a long time ago, before my father left us and moved in with his girlfriend, Amy, who's from Australia. Have you ever heard a Chinese person speak with an Australian accent? It's weird, but that's not the only reason I hate her.

Leaving my house is the best part of going to school.

The clouds are dark grey and low in the sky today, so low that they seem to be converging on the roofs of the houses, curling around the chimneys, leaving fine drops of water that coat the eaves and shingles. The buds are just forming on the branches of the cherry trees that run down the left side of the sidewalk. I smell rain. It's unmistakable, that smell, like ocean and ozone and springtime. I think of it as the smell of this city, the thing that makes Vancouver different from every other city in the world. Not that I would know, I've only ever been to Seattle, and that place smells exactly the same.

It's three blocks to the bus stop, the same three blocks I've been walking since I started going to high school. We've lived in this neighbourhood on the East Side in the same house since before I was born. Everyone knows us here. Mrs. Bianchi lives on the corner and every summer gives us romaine lettuce and green peppers from her garden. The Millbanks are the people in the old character house with the huge horse chestnut tree. And Mr. and Mrs. Wong, we've known them the longest. Mrs. Wong asked my mom to go on an Alaskan cruise with her last year, but my mother said she couldn't because I was still too young to be left alone. But really, I think it's because we don't have a lot of money. My father sends us cheques every month and the house is paid for, but there's never anything left over for extras, like real haircuts or the jeans that everyone else is buying at school. When he left, no one asked us any questions, but I saw Mrs. Bianchi bringing in our empty trash cans on garbage collection day and Mr. Wong fixed the leaking gutter without even being asked. When you live with the same people for years and years, things don't need to be explained. You start to understand the pulse of the other families, and you know when something's wrong, when silence envelops a house so tightly not a sound escapes and no new sounds can ever leak in.

I walk past the small rental house with the blue paint peeling off the siding. The front door is open and I can see into the hall. It looks dark inside, as if the walls were once white but have slowly absorbed years of dirt and smog and cigarette smoke. Even the windows are covered in a thin layer of brown film, dense in some spots, transparent in others. A black cat with a white stripe down its face crouches on the front step, its head tensed and eyes pale in this grey morning light. Cats give me the creeps, especially in the spring, when every animal seems crazier than usual. I shudder a little and zip my jacket up past my chin.

I'm still staring at the cat when a tall figure steps through the hall and out the front door. He wears a red jacket and a pair of baggy jeans and he jingles a ring of keys in his hand. I must look stupid, mouth half-hidden in my collar, head turned to gape at his unnerving, unblinking cat. I trip on a tree root that has started to crack open the sidewalk, which is the most ridiculous thing to do, because that tree root has been there for as long as I can remember and I've never, not even once, stumbled on it. I'm arms out like a kid playing airplane, one leg up, and I take five awkward, could-be-drunk steps until I come to a jerky full stop on the grass. I want to die.

(The last time I saw him, sometime in the fall, I was walking home after going out for a birthday dinner with Anna Bianchi and some other friends from the neighbourhood. He was sitting on a blanket spread on the damp lawn with his roommates, drinking beer and playing music on a portable stereo. He didn't see me then, because it was dark out and I kept to the other side of the street, but I was looking at him. He sat in the grass like he had been doing it his whole life, like he was born in a meadow in this same precise hour just after twilight, like this one moment with his friends was all he was thinking about, and not yesterday or the next week or about how he was going to finish all the things that he was supposed to. All that existed for him was this cold night, this nodding of his blond head at his bearded roommate who was talking about cognitive science and his new lady professor who was so flawlessly beautiful he barely remembered anything that came out of her perfect mouth. *I could talk to them*, I thought.)

I hope he doesn't see me. Maybe if I stand perfectly still, I'll look like a tree trunk or a lamp post. He looks up, and I close my eyes against that sharp jaw that means he's not a boy like all the boys I know, but a boy who just became a man who no longer remembers what high school was even like.

I can't stand here forever with my eyes closed like this. But I can't decide if this not moving thing is more stupid or if walking toward the bus stop like nothing happened is worse.

I open my eyes.

He stands on the concrete walk to his house and looks at me with his head cocked. I notice for the first time that his eyes are brown, which somehow surprises me. He's seeing me—there's no question—but his gaze is like a tickle, a barely there touch that grazes the tips of my ears and the line of my jaw. Not invasive at all. Maybe even just short of genius. I sniff. The rain is getting closer.

"Stopping to smell the roses?" he asks me. How is it possible that he's speaking to me, that his voice is running down the back of my neck like melted chocolate? I shift my knapsack and take a step backward.

"Yeah. Sure. The roses." I've only repeated what he just said even though there are no roses, only daffodils that haven't bloomed yet. He'll think I have a disability. I should definitely start walking to the bus stop. I look like a stalker, standing here on this guy's front lawn. But he isn't yelling at me to go away, so maybe he doesn't mind.

I take three steps forward and I can hear him unlocking his car door behind me. Good, this whole incident is over and I can get on with my life, maybe finally catch a bus and go to school, like I'm supposed to, like every other day when absolutely nothing happens. But then, he speaks.

"What's your name?"

I turn around and he's smiling at me, leaning with his elbow on the roof of his car. If I ran toward him and threw my arms around his neck, would that be too much? I picture us holding hands and walking down the beach, with his cat on a leash beside us. Waves drift in gently around our feet. I shake my head. Focus. I have to focus.

"Margaret," I say, too loudly and too quickly to be anything but an idiot.

"I'm Grant. It's nice to meet you." And he winks at me before he ducks into the car.

The rest of the walk is like looking through a smudge of grease on glass. I see the trees and houses, but they're blurry, like dream trees and dream houses. All I hear is a loud pounding between my temples that sounds like "he saw me—he loves me—he saw me—he loves me." My steps fall into the same rhythm and I'm half-convinced that our love is real. If I could, I would hug myself.

When I'm finally on the bus, I'm not even sure how I got here, whether I showed the driver my pass or if I just lurched up the stairs and found a seat. My head feels gummy and heavy and I need some quiet time to breathe it all out. It's a good thing, for today anyway, that the ride is so long and that my brother forced me to go to a school across the city near the university. At the time, when I was getting ready to go into grade eight, he told me that I needed to meet new people for networking purposes. I guess networking with Anna Bianchi at the local East Side high school wasn't what he had in mind.

The bus is foggy this morning. The damp breath of all these people has collected on the windows and water runs down the glass. I always feel itchy on the bus, as if bugs are crawling off other people's bodies and are making their way toward me. I can smell that someone in the back has been drinking all night and has probably peed on himself at least once. I look out the window at Broadway, at the shops that change slowly as we inch west. At first, it's ninety-nine cent pizza shops and lowrise apartment buildings with blackout curtains in the windows. Then, the neon sign of a DVD store flashes blue and red and green, one colour after another, and we pass a laundry where the clothes must be dirtier coming out than going in. Today, there's only one prostitute still leaning against the exterior wall of the corner store that sells fried chicken. She turns her head slowly as the bus rolls past and she blinks, as if this is the first time she's considered that it might be morning already.

Main Street sneaks up on me; it just appears out of nothing. All of a sudden, I'm no longer passing Vietnamese diners and an orange-brick strip mall. All of a sudden, this is *Main Street*, all designer shops and urban grime. A couple sips coffee at an outdoor table, the woman wearing a tight jacket and the man in vintage glasses. They both look ironic and skinny and I think that they must be trying so hard to make it seem as if being ironic and skinny are not things they aspire to, but things they just are. Maybe I could do that someday, sit at a Main Street hipster café with someone (with Grant maybe, except I'm trying to forget him so I don't obsess and obsess about him saying eight words to me that mean nothing, but could mean everything), except, eventually, everyone would figure out that my irony and skinniness are an outside layer, and that, inside, I'm just Margaret Tan, naturally knock-kneed and still scared of ghosts. Not interesting at all. Less than boring. Someone you would never even notice.

It was only last night that I stayed up late watching *Mystic Pizza* on TV and by the end of the movie, after Cat has totally figured out that the man she babysits for was never in love with her, I thought I felt something soft brush the back of my neck, like the end of a scarf or strands of fine, little girl hair. Maybe it's normal to feel touches you can't explain, by people or creatures you can never see. I don't care because it sure didn't feel normal to me. The word *ghost* echoed in my head, bouncing and multiplying until that was all I could think of. That's when I closed my eyes and ran to my bedroom and stuffed a quilt in the crack under the door. I lay awake for hours and hours, but never opened my eyes once. I only fell asleep when I heard my mother tiptoe to the washroom and I drifted off to the sound of her pee hitting the water in the toilet.

I'm halfway to school. Still twenty more minutes to go before I step through those double doors, painted a dull green, like mould on cheese. No rain yet, just that flat blanket of dark clouds.

I don't hate school. I'm in advanced classes for most things (except math and chemistry—whoever said that Chinese people are good at numbers has obviously never met me) and I like that feeling of being consumed by what you're reading or listening to, like all the brain cells in your head are working at full capacity. You don't know if you can handle it, but then you always do. Each classroom is a square of isolation, where nothing outside matters inside.

The hallways are the worst part, having to walk through crowds of kids who might be looking at me or might not, whose clothes are more expensive than mine. Even though I know there's nothing I can do about it, the rest of them just think that I dress this way because I'm too stupid to know any better. I wear my brother's old jeans and shrunken patterned thrift-shop sweaters that old men probably used to wear, you know, the kind with checks and diagonal stripes and triangles. I like hats. I have a whole plastic tub of different kinds of hats that I find at yard sales and in my friends' basements. Today, I'm wearing a blue cloche that Anna's grandmother gave me when I visited last weekend.

All those eyes. I've been at this school for three years and the eyes still seem so unreal to me, the way they float over things, not pausing any longer to consider me or the banner hanging from the ceiling advertising the Spring Fling Dance. When I came here, I thought that there would be more kids like me, the ones who bus across the city far away from what their parents are so scared of (namely, bunches of teenagers roaming the streets at night with nothing to do but break into cars, sniff glue and get pregnant). But, as it turns out, in my grade, there are only five or six of us from the East Side and they're all invisible. They don't carry the marks of their neighbourhoods on them. Things like home-cut hair, dresses for special occasions that don't quite fit because they're someone else's, drugstore eye shadow that creases on the lids.

It's easy to see me once and think you know my story. Chinese girl who's good at school, whose parents never let her do anything but study, who doesn't even care about how she looks. Partly true, but also not true at all.

Mostly, I just wish you couldn't see me at all.

Unless you're Grant (who is in my head again, although I'm making a promise to myself that this is the *very last time*).

At Granville Street, everything changes again. There's that big bookstore on the corner, all glass, and a row of art galleries running north, the kind that are only good to look at through the windows. It's early still and people aren't shopping yet, only hurrying through the crosswalks, streaming in and out of the bank, their shiny leather shoes hitting the pavement as if they're beating it into submission. A car signals left—a dark, sleek, low car that looks like it might purr instead of growl. Everyone on the bus turns to look at it, at how perfect and shiny it is, at the shadowy driver behind the tinted glass who may not be as perfect as the car but whom we all imagine to be anyway.

Up the street, just fifteen blocks or so south, is where all the big, old houses are. The last time I went trick-or-treating, my brother took me there, saying, "They'll have better candy, Mags, and we'll get to see inside." He was more excited than I was.

What I remember most was the light. The windows glowed when I looked at them from the outside, and it wasn't just one or two windows, but all of them, the ones on the upper floors, even the ones on the sides. I thought about home, where we turned off every light when we left a room, about how my father used to scream at us if we forgot. "Electricity isn't free, for crying out loud," he'd shout from wherever he was without even looking to see if it was me or my brother.

And those big houses were warm too. I could feel the puffs of heated air on my cheeks as I waited for the candy. At one house, a little girl about my age stood behind her father as he blithered about the creativity of my costume (that year, I went as a Christmas tree, which meant my brother and I made a poncho of green felt and taped ornaments and tinsel all over it and I wore a hat with a tin foil star standing crookedly on the top of my head) and I could see that she was only wearing a hula girl costume with a tank top and grass skirt. That night, the mist was sharp, burrowing its way into the neck of my costume and up my sleeves, biting my skin whenever it made contact. All that October, I had been wearing two layers minimum in the house because my father refused to turn on the heat until the middle of November on principle and, even then, the tip of my nose was cold to the touch and I had to pull my sleeves over my hands. The girl just stood there in the marble-tiled hall in her bare feet and stared at me. It was hard to turn around and walk back into the chilly night with my brother, who muttered about property values and municipal taxes. "That house will be mine one day," he said to the windshield. "I'm not sweating over this MBA for nothing." At least he didn't expect me to listen.

We're at MacDonald now and an old woman is getting on, her arms shaking as she pushes her walker forward, her glasses sliding down her nose millimetre by millimetre. I stand up and offer her my seat and she nods before collapsing into a small pile of herringbone tweed. I wonder if she's made up of only bones and fabric and hair, the flesh—after years of moving and scratching and maybe even babies—thin and stretched and flaking away every time she moves.

My mother doesn't look much different. Empty of weight. Putting in time until time is up.

The old woman smiles at me as the bus swerves around an illegally parked car outside a two-storey clothing store. When she speaks her voice is loud, nothing like the dry whisper I was expecting.

"Thank you," she says. "It's very nice of you."

I don't really like old people—it's that smell of medicinal creams that treat growths and rashes I'd rather not know about, and their fragility, as if a hearty laugh could rip them in half and leave nothing behind but traces of dust and maybe their bifocals. But she seems like a nice lady and the bus is too crowded now for me to move to the back or ignore her completely.

"You're welcome," I say and I smile back.

The bus swerves again into the right lane and the old lady's lavender crochet bag falls to the floor. Pill bottles and makeup and loose change and books of stamps spill out and begin rolling around and under the feet of the other passengers.

"Oh no," she gasps as she waves her hands in the air.

I stoop down and pick up her things, muttering "excuse me" to the legs around me. I even manage to stop a roll of blackcurrant jellies from falling through a crack in the rear door. As I hand it all back to her (she's smiling sheepishly and the tips of her ears are red), I see that I've scooped up a crumpled brochure and am still holding it in my left hand.

On the front, there's only one line in capital letters: THE TIME IS NEAR. Behind the words, a swirling cloud that is equal parts black and grey and red and orange seems to come at me, as if determined to explode off this piece of paper and into the real-world air. A giant alarm clock floats in the middle, its hands at five to twelve; noon or midnight, there's no way to tell and, for some reason, this freaks me out more. What's worse? A daytime Armageddon that envelops a blue sky with clouds like these? Or one that violently pushes you from sleep to waking and there's no time to change? What if I couldn't check on my mother? What if my father didn't bother to check on me?

The old woman leans forward and touches my arm with her fingertips. I shiver. "You can keep that, my dear, as a thank you." She stuffs a small plastic bag of cotton balls into the bottom of her purse. "Since we're here together, let me ask you a question. If the end came now, would you be satisfied with the way you've lived your life?"

If I were a different sort of person, I would say to her, What kind of question is that to ask a sixteen-year-old girl? A girl who fell in love with her neighbour just thirty-five minutes ago? Whose mother hasn't looked her in the eye for four years? The way she's lived her life, you dried-up piece of lady jerky, has nothing at all to do with choices, so what satisfaction can there be in that? Being satisfied has nothing to do with it. Only survival and even that isn't so much of a choice. She breathes because that's what humans do, one set of inhale and exhale after another. You can stuff your brochure, you witch-eyed fanatic, and leave me alone.

It takes me only seven seconds to think all this. Meanwhile, she stares at me with eyes that eat up two thirds of her face and blinks, dispersing the pools of water that collect in the bottom lids. She's leaking fluid constantly. No wonder she's so small.

But I have to say something, so I pull my arm away from her touch and mutter, "I suppose."

"That's not good enough. You can't just suppose when the Lord is asking you about your sins." She straightens up and shakes her head. "There's no more certainty these days when it comes to good and bad. People spend too much time thinking about their own material problems and not enough about their souls and the souls of others. Navel gazing, as my son would say."

She doesn't read minds. That's not possible. But I feel as guilty as if she had.

"But we really don't have to worry about anything except how we conduct ourselves and choosing the right thing to do over the wrong thing. My rule," she says, pressing a hand to her chest, "is to hurt no one's feelings and to tell the truth as kindly as you can."

"But the truth isn't always kind," I blurt, before I even have time to think. I should know better than to engage in conversation with a woman who gives out Armageddon brochures instead of thank you cards.

She squints at me as if she's seeing me in a new way. Then again, maybe she just needs stronger glasses. "You're right. The truth can be terrible. But without truth, we're just living in a fog, don't you think?"

A fog. Like the fog my mother walks and sits and sleeps in. For the first time, I wonder if she even believes my father has left us, if she really understands that there actually is a woman named Amy who now claims him as hers. Or if she thinks he's still her husband and he's going to come home tonight, even though he hasn't visited us in three years. If that fog that breathes with her is necessary because, otherwise, she would see what our life really is, which is the two of us together, thin and mostly silent.

And that house, unchanged for as long as I can remember, except for those times when my father and then my brother moved out. They left behind old versions of themselves that cling to the cobwebs in the corners like sloughed-off skin, transparent and thin, ghostly even. Maybe, eventually, I won't be able to tell my mother from the ghosts or from my own reflection in the mirror.

The old lady shakes her head as the bus bounces through a pothole. The curls on the top of her head shake too. "The only real ghost is the Holy Ghost, my dear."

I stare at her, at the grey-blue eyes that might once have been a deeper colour, at the skin on her neck that pulls and bags at the same time. I don't know what to say to her. The lights in the bus flicker and I think that she will disappear in the brief dim and I will never see her again, but when the lights come back on, she's still sitting there, looking at me, waiting for me to say something.

"I don't believe in ghosts," I say, because I can't think of anything else.

She pulls out a pair of pink leather gloves from her coat pocket and slides her hands into them. "In my experience, ghosts are nothing more than the things we haven't let go of yet. When my husband died, I thought I could smell the smoke from his cigars every time I stepped out on to the porch and I started to believe he was still alive. But he wasn't, you know, I just didn't want to face it. Then, one day, the smoke was gone."

She grabs the support pole and begins to haul herself up. I take her elbow and steady her against the shake and tilt of the speeding bus. As she stands, she turns her face to the open window and sniffs. "It smells like rain, don't you think?" And she totters off, pushing the walker ahead of her.

I stand there, staring at car after car after car. I feel buried underneath the mess in my head. I'm not really confused, only terribly tired, as if my throat is full of rocks and my body is struggling to breathe and move the blood from vein to heart and out again. I turn to the window and blink hard, but I'm still on Broadway, still inside this bus with an ad for a herpes clinic above my head. A man in a red track suit bumps into me and it's like an electric shock, the feel of someone else's warm body, the pressure of his flesh. I can't remember the last time my mother hugged me so hard I could feel her hot breath on my ear and the squeeze of her arms around my shoulders. Or the last time I heard my father's voice, which is somehow always tinny and broken, as if the line we're talking on is going to die any minute and there will soon be nothing, just me saying, "Hello? Hello," over and over again, throwing that one word into a sea of crackling silence.

Maybe Grant will want to hold me, the air between us like compressed heat, no ghostly voices in the room, only our own—real-life, lung-powered, so tangible we can practically see them without ever taking our eyes off each other.

The street widens to the grassy boulevard that marks the campus of the university and my high school. I pick up my backpack and step off the bus. As soon as I cross the street, the noise changes. It's as if the trees swallow the sounds of traffic and all I can hear are my footsteps and the shifting of books inside my bag. This is the best part of going to school here, I think, being cocooned by green and the sensation that I'm all alone in this damp, soft place, the kind of place that doesn't exist in the neighbourhood we live in.

There's no such thing as quiet there, only parks dotted with empty concrete wading pools and bordered on all sides by busy streets and the heavy smell of cooking oil that floats out of kitchen windows at dinnertime. I realize that the peace here might be a fancy illusion; after all, every family, west side or not, has its problems, right? I look up at a house perched on a hill, a house with floor to ceiling windows and a flat roof. I can see everything: the sleek, white chairs, the pale wood coffee table, even through the patio door and into the back garden. Maybe the people who live there are so happy, it doesn't matter if their neighbours can see everything. Or maybe they live like everyone else—crying and screaming and ignoring each other when they've run out of words—but don't care what the outside world thinks because the outside world is just that. Outside.

It would just be you and your family, seeing each other all the time because there are no walls, just open space and glass, and light in all corners to illuminate the solidity of your cheeks and elbows and hair. It would be impossible to hate a house like that.

I stand at the doors to the school, green like always, scarred with use and overuse. Inside, the same girls in the same clothes are probably already huddled in groups by their lockers, with the boys leaning against the walls like they don't even care that the girls look at them and titter. It'll be a day like yesterday, but maybe not quite.

I reach out to open the door and a cool wind breathes into the back of my neck. Finally, it's starting to rain.

Family Parade
Gul Joya Jafri

The household is in a state of chaos.

My mother rushes around the kitchen grabbing tin foil, plastic wrap and lunch bags for the aloo-chutney sandwiches spread in rows on the kitchen table.

"Oh *Ji*," she shouts to my father, who is running up and down stairs gathering picnic supplies. "Can you get my purse from the closet? And grab my sunglasses too!"

My little sister Anika bounces a rubber ball along the kitchen walls yelling "Orange! Crush! Pepsi!"—with a loud thump following each exclamation—in imitation of a game I gave up playing last year. As usual, she forgets to say "Cola!" at the end.

Meanwhile, my grandmother shuffles down the hallway, lamenting her aching bones a bit more loudly than usual, and mutters about going out in hot weather. And my aunt and cousins, who have just arrived, talk all at once in the entryway, urging us *"Chalo! Chalo!"*—hurry up—so that we will not be late for the parade.

Upstairs, I am seated on my bed, arms crossed, tapping my heels with impatience. I have been waiting to use the bathroom down the hall, which my grandfather has occupied for the last half hour. I suspect that he is cleaning his toenails—he refuses to put on his sandals without this ritual.

I sigh. I didn't really want to go to the parade in the first place, at least not with my family. But most of my friends are away on vacation or working summer jobs. We hardly ever go on vacation; the last real trip was to visit relatives in Pakistan, over three years ago. Instead, I think sullenly, we go on dumb family trips downtown, even if it takes forever to drive there.

"ALIYA!" I hear the sharpness in my mother's voice as it carries through the hallway and up the stairs.

"WHAT?" I shout back, not moving.

"GET DOWN HERE AND HELP YOUR FATHER CARRY THE FOOD TO THE CAR. WE'RE LEAVING!"

"I can't go! Someone's in the bathroom, I can't get ready!"

"So? Go use the other one. You have five minutes," my mother snaps.

Before I am able to retort that all my things are in THIS one, I hear the bathroom door open as my grandfather steps out. I jump up and sprint down the hallway, nearly tripping at the bathroom entrance, and blurt out "Feew, gross!" as I spot a stray toenail in the bathroom sink. I gingerly pick it out with a piece of toilet paper. That is when I see my reflection in the mirror, and my already foul mood plummets. My hair refused to obey my commands this morning, and now there are strands curling and frizzing in odd directions. Worst of all, there is a new pimple on my nose.

Maybe it is just as well that I am not heading to the mall with my friend Farah, who got back last week from her family trip to Kenya. At least downtown, I won't have to worry about running into anyone I know.

Hurriedly I splash water on my face, wipe it dry and rub some Clearasil on the embarrassing zit, squirming at the image in the mirror. My eyes are okay, but my nose and lips are so big. And my skin just seems to get darker each summer. I had better pick up some sunscreen at the—

"ALIYA! WHERE ARE YOU?" At the sound of my mother's voice, I quickly tie back my hair and run downstairs.

Ten minutes later, I am seated in the "kids car," driven by my father, as he tries to navigate the weekend traffic on the Don Valley Parkway. My two cousins, whom everyone refers to as the Twins because they are only a year apart and look so much alike, are seated on either side of Anika, who is singing a garbled version of the ABCs. I expel a loud breath and try to fan my face. It is sticky and hot, I am stuck with a bunch of little kids, and my dad has launched into a history lesson about the Caribbean—something about sugar plantations, which I tune out. I look terrible. Worse, my mom didn't wash my favourite Cotton Ginny T-shirt yet, and I have to wear another one that I now realize smells of the past week's cooking.

It is a full forty-five minutes before we reach downtown. My father instructs me to keep a lookout for parking, as he checks to see that my aunt's car, in which my mother and grandparents are seated, is right behind us.

"How come it's always so crowded and busy downtown?" I ask grumpily. However, just as he begins a lecture about urban development and summer festivals, I spot a large handwritten poster reading "Welcome to Caribana '87! For Parking—Turn Left" and interrupt him to follow the signs.

I can already hear the echoes of steel drums accompanied by a heavy bass beat as we begin to walk over to University Avenue. It lends an air of energy and excitement to the city and I start to feel more optimistic about the outing.

The Twins try to grab my arms—my hands are full, carrying bags of sandwiches and fruit—and pull me forward, chattering excitedly as they debate whether this parade will be like the one we saw on Canada Day, although we arrived late and missed most of it. My grandfather follows behind, prayer mat under one arm, video camera in the other. He keeps adjusting the camera as he walks along, calling out to us to pose for him at each streetlight, with periodic shouts of, *"Bachcha* party! Wave to Dada! Hel-lo! Hel-lo!"

The others straggle behind with my grandmother, who shuffles forward slowly, stopping occasionally to rub her back.

We squeeze through crowds of people sporting bikini tops, shorts, sandals and sunglasses, some cheering for their favourite floats, most shaking their jiggly body parts, in rhythm and off rhythm to the thumping beats. With my mother shouting from behind for everyone to stay together, we manage to find a shady spot from which we can see the parade. Dark-skinned, bare-chested men in red and black headbands float past on a truck playing steel drums, and children decked out in costumes with coloured feathers and strands of sequins expertly move along beside them, blowing on whistles to the beat.

I am mesmerized, however, by the blinding and provocative costumes worn by the women—tidbits of cloth covering breasts and hips in the brightest pinks, blues and yellows.

The beat is deafening, and infectious. I want to dance, but don't know how, and glance enviously at a pale blond girl, coconut sunscreen melting down her face, who dances to this music as though she's done it all her life. I wonder if I could at least sway to the beat, without getting lectured by my mother or grandmother. Apart from the Twins and my sister, who are jumping about and pointing to their favourite costumes, everyone else in the family stands still, observing the carefree dancing with serious attention. My grandmother has already begun her expected tirade about the debauchery she is being forced to observe.

"Hai, Allah preserve us," she says, automatically adjusting her large white dupatta to cover her head fully. "This music is too loud, I'm going to

go deaf. And these people have no shame at all." At this, she points a finger into the parade. "Look at that woman's costume, there is nothing hidden from view!"

We all glance over to see a slim black woman wearing an elaborate, sparkling silver headpiece, with matching sequins barely covering her breasts, and silver lamé hot pants. She shakes her hips and winks at my grandfather, who is following her movements with his video camera as she passes by.

"What do you expect from these people, they were all slaves. Let them celebrate their freedom!" he retorts, and continues to videotape the event.

I feel relieved that no one in the crowd arround us appears to understand Urdu.

After a few minutes of fidgeting and trying to keep myself from moving to the music, I decide that I need to take action. The kids are playing a game of spotting costumes, my grandfather is busy with his videotaping, and my mother and grandmother are once again counselling my aunt on how to deal with her husband, who never seems to be home and whom she keeps threatening to divorce. Only my father looks tired and lost in thought, not really seeing the parade. This is boring. Everyone else around us is having fun, and I want to have fun, too.

"I'm going to go watch the parade from that corner," I tell my mother. "It's less crowded."

She stops speaking to my aunt and glances over to where I am pointing. "There's no shade over there. You'll get dark," she cautions. "Here. Wear this." She removes the Canadian Tire visor she'd been wearing and gives it to me. I say nothing, but resolve to take it off as soon as I am out of sight.

Before I can escape, Anika takes my hand, exclaiming that she wants to wear the visor too. My mother calls out, "Take your sister with you!"

With a sigh, I pick out some food to bring along and pass the ugly visor to Anika, who happily sticks it on her head even though it is too big.

Finally, from my new location, I begin to enjoy the parade. Luckily my sister is not whiny yet and, grabbing her little hands, I swing her arms back and forth, occasionally pointing to interesting floats and costumes as they go by. Dancing with her, I don't care as much if I look silly—and when Anika begins to sway her hips, I do the same.

Eventually, the aroma of barbecued hot dogs reaches my nose and my stomach growls in response. Anika notices my stare in the direction of the hot dog stand and begins to jump up and down, exclaiming, "I want hot dog! Hot dog!"

I take on a stern expression to convince her this is not a good idea. "*Chi-chi*. Hot dogs are yucky. Full of pork." Instead, I push an aloo-chutney sandwich, now soggy from the chutney and oil, into her hands. She looks down at it and wrinkles her nose, shaking her head.

At that moment, I feel a tap on my shoulder. "Aliya?"

I turn around and gasp in surprise. It's David Ali, one of the cutest guys from school, who was in my history class last year. I really like him, but we never get much of a chance to talk—he's always with his friends, and I've been too shy to just go up to him and start a conversation.

"David! What are you doing here?" I ask, then look down at his feet realizing what a dumb question that is. I am trying to absorb the shock of seeing him and simultaneously worrying about how awful my hair must look and whether he can see the pimple from this angle.

"Uh, I came down with some of my brother's friends," he says, nodding toward a group of guys jumping up and down to the reggae rhythms coming from the float passing us by. "I, um, was just heading over there to get a hot dog." He pauses, adjusting his sunglasses, then clears his throat. "How about you?"

"Oh, um, yeah. I, er, came with some cousins," I say, gesturing vaguely behind me, figuring that it is not a compete lie. I am relieved that he can't see my family, staring statue-like at the lively spectacle.

He nods, looking behind me with some puzzlement, then goes on to make conversation about his summer activities. I chat with him happily, feeling thrilled that the boring family trip has brought about such an exciting event. I can't wait to get home and share every detail with Farah.

After several minutes of conversation, David shuffles his feet and says he should probably get back to his group. With a wave goodbye, he asks, "See you next month at school?"

I nod blissfully, already imagining the two of us as a couple. With the loud beat reverberating in my ears, I feel a burst of energy and spin around to grab my sister and dance in celebration.

Except that she is no longer standing next to me. I look around quickly, left, right, behind me—she is not there. My heart begins to pound loudly and I feel panic and fear rush through me. My thoughts are racing and I try to calm myself. Surely she is nearby. She probably got bored while I was talking and wanted to go back to our family, although they are several feet away and not in plain view. I walk back toward them, slowly looking around in case she has gone in the wrong direction, until my family is in full sight. The fear takes complete hold of me now. My sister is not with them. Worse, my mother has spotted me alone, without Anika.

"Where is Anika?" she demands.

I gulp. "Um…she was right next to me. I swear. She was right there. She must be nearby. I'll find her."

I can see the anger and worry in my mother's eyes. "What do you mean? She's lost? I ask you to take care of your sister for ten minutes and you can't even do that?" My mother begins to scan the crowd and calls out to my father, aunt and grandfather that Anika is lost and that everyone should start searching for her.

"Stay here and take care of your grandmother," orders my mother. "And make sure you don't lose her, too," she adds tartly. The spectators standing near us turn at the commotion, wondering what is going on.

By now I am ready to cry. My grandmother has begun to detail all the gruesome scenarios. "Hai, Allah forbid anything should have happened to your sister. Just last night I heard on the news about a child who was kidnapped from a city park. And there are so many people here. Anyone could have grabbed her and no one would even notice. Or what if she wandered into the traffic? There are so many cars nearby..."

I desperately try to tune out her dramatic commentary, along with the cacophony of music and laughter that are now heightening my own anxiety. I try to concentrate, and to think where Anika might have wandered. Standing on tiptoe, I look around above the heads of thousands of spectators, hoping I can spot a glimpse of my little sister in her pink dress. But there are too many people all dressed in bright colours, all moving in a blur.

Suddenly I remember the hot dogs. Maybe Anika wandered over to the hot dog stand? I search for one of the adults to tell them to check over there, but none is in hearing range as they wander through the crowds trying to find Anika.

"Amma, I'll be back in two minutes," I say to my grandmother and push past some spectators, from whom I get dirty looks in my haste to reach the hot dog stand. I am convinced that this is where Anika must have gone and begin to feel hopeful.

She isn't there. The hot dog vendor squints in curiosity—he can probably see the disappointment on my face. Before I can ask him anything however, a young couple with an infant arrives and orders two hot dogs. I rush back to where I left my grandmother, hoping that I have not lost her, too.

Luckily, my grandmother is still there, and she is waving madly at something in the parade when I reach her. "It's Anika! Look! There she is! Anika is in the parade! She just waved at me!"

I look toward the parade. A calypso float, with the words, "Island Chutney" emblazoned in bright red across the front, is going by. A West Indian girl in a fluffy pink dress, about Anika's age, is jubilantly dancing about and waving sporadically to the crowd.

"*Amma*, that's not Anika. That's another girl. Anika was wearing a pink dress, remember?"

My grandmother expels her breath in frustration. "*Aré*, no one ever listens to me! I told you, I saw her, she was in the parade, she just went by. Walk down further that way, you'll see her."

Feeling doubtful, I begin to walk in that direction when my grandmother shouts again. "Look! On the other side! It's Anika!"

I look over across the parade and, indeed, it is Anika, smiling, waving and being carried on the shoulders of a tall black man wearing a bright orange, sleeveless tee covered with a green and black flag with a yellow "X" emblazoned across it. She has stuck the Canadian Tire visor on his head, and I can't help noting that it suits him much better. In any case, it is clear to me that he is carrying Anika through the parade and past the crowds in the hopes that she will be spotted by her family.

I join my grandmother in shouting and waving at him, no longer caring who is turning around to stare at us. My mother, who is walking back toward us, sees what we are pointing to and squeezes past the parade barricades to reach the other side, and is nearly knocked over by a mammoth set of sparkling purple butterfly wings. She grabs Anika from the man, who appears to be trying to explain where he found her. My mother nods brusquely, muttering a few words in response. At the first gap between floats, she rushes back with Anika to where we are waiting. I wonder if she even thanked the man.

Half an hour later, we trudge back toward the parking lot to head home, after nearly losing my grandfather too, who had given up searching for Anika and went to pray for her on a nearby patch of grass instead. No one wants to talk, except the Twins, who are now harassing my aunt about why we haven't had a picnic and eaten all the food we brought with us. Anika, it turns out, did indeed wander over near the hot dog stand, where the man found her, crying. My mother has not said a word to me, but through her stony silence I can feel her anger. I am sure I will be subjected to a lecture after my aunt has gone home, and that I will be hearing about this incident for several weeks to come.

My single source of relief is that my mother does not know I was distracted because of a boy—and worse, I realize suddenly, a boy who happens to be black.

Poems
Moez Surani

81

CLINTON STREET POEM

Dear God,
could you move the sun?
It's in the painter's eyes.

DREAM SONG

*"Put on your good shirt, Mr. Bones,
we's goin to the ballgame!"*

(UNTITLED)

I meet her in the driveway.

Hugging her in front of her car,
she asks if I can drive. Then, leaning

over the gear shift and parking brake,
hugs me again.

Grieving Clara.

LEONARD COHEN

After looking into his cereal spoon,
Leonard Cohen knocked over the chair. Backing away from the table.

He saw himself in the dense angle. Opening the cupboard, he saw himself
spread over curved metal soup tins.

PACKING FOR MONTREAL

In the kitchen fruit basket the apples,
wrapped in their red and green dirges,
are upset that I am leaving.
They have been ignoring me.

Last night,
how quickly we moved apart.
A handshake, one friend ducking
into a cab that descended like an arrow
down Yonge Street.
We took another one north
a handshake in my driveway.
With our different universities
we've done this
a hundred times.

Men departing without histrionics.

I leave only absurd
sentimental fruit behind.

Poems
Tanya Bryan

85

TRANSI(EN)T LOVE

another night on the 504
while away the time watching
the sidewalk crawl beside me

I saw the worn leather boots first
pumping to reach their stop
ahead of my streetcar

black and silver boots running
as the metal beast clacks along
he barely makes it

"thank you" his thick Scottish accent
tumbles through the car at me
and I'm in love with a punk rock boy

his spiky black hair points upward
punching and puncturing the ceiling
mutiny against nature and gravity

how does he keep his foot-long hair up?
with an iron and glue, like his forefathers,
or hairspray and sheer rebel will?

his faded black jeans, ripped and badly pinned,
reveal strong legs stopping two seats ahead
I look away so he doesn't know I stare

he sits, the green monster's hand on the back
of his patchy leather jacket gives the finger
but I know it isn't meant for me

his music fills the almost-empty car
The Clash pounds past like it's 1979
as we continue east on King towards 2009

he blows on his exposed fingers
poking out from his hobo-style gloves
made popular by many before him

he tugs the cord at Bathurst, ambles my way
I give him a two-fingered punk rock salute
as he takes the steps two at a time into the past

SPACE FILLER

you'd think we knew each other
in front of that bank on Bloor West
the way he snugged in so tight
his arm sashaying about my shoulders
natural as a boa on Elton John
nospacebetween

but he was filler
picture 36 on a roll of 37
disposable

DO NOT FEED THE ANIMALS

The elephants and monkeys moved to Scarborough in 1974
leaving the Clydesdales, sheep, chickens and pigs behind
Riverdale Farm, animal anomaly once the norm in Toronto,
nestled like a chicken's egg in Cabbagetown padded
by the Victorian houses where the poor Irish immigrants
supposedly grew cabbage in their front yards
cows are milked next to where William Lyon Mackenzie lies

A father and children feed the goats a fallen branch
the children laugh as the goats clamber and leap
to munch on the extended leafy treat until it's gone
the children pull, yank and twist on a live tree
wrestling for more fodder
the angry farmer orders them to read the sign at every pen:
Do Not Feed The Animals
which can encourage aggressive behaviour
and discourage consumption of their controlled nutritional feed
father feigns innocence, ignorance,
leaves his children to their berating
the children leave the goats to their bleating
and start throwing grass at the sad donkey

Church and Gerrard
Maria Corbett

There is a hum. Surrounding me Toronto respires. It gapes. Gap toothed to the world. I imagine a yawning crater sucking anything that isn't nailed down into itself. Feeding. Feeding off the teaming life scurrying at its feet. Feeding off me. All around skyscrapers stand their ground. Like giant teeth. Proud. Immovable. Unchanging. Blank faced. I am being eaten alive by this city, sucked dry, desiccated in the dead heat, desiccated in the aircon. Moving around like a cell in an artery. It diminishes me and I give it life.

I stand at the window and look east. My first morning back in Toronto, I was here at six. Wide awake from jetlag, I watched the sunrise. First the neon orange glow, then the pink, seeping gloriously into the light blue predawn sky. The colour of his eyes. Blue and white and green and yellow, watercolour strength. The ambient glow stole westward, touched and lightly caressed the sleeping city, nudging warmly at the corners of buildings, like a lover coming to bed long after you've been asleep. Touching you gently with his body, kissing the side of your face and the matted hair pushed onto your cheek by the night, cupping your body with his, shielding and protecting you, trying not to wake you but finding he has, pulling you closer and breathing you in.

He used to come to me like this from work. Stealing quietly into his bed. Curving around me, soft skin on soft skin. I would smell the sweat, the bar, the booze, the smoke, sticky all over him. If he wasn't very gentle, I knew he wanted me awake and I would oblige, stretching into him, fitting his body as I was made to do. Running my hand along his back, it would catch on the film covering him. Smelling his hair, same texture as during the day, different scent. Trying to find him I'd search for his mouth in the dark. He would look for me too. Tongues would touch. Mouths would meet. Hunger moved us and we would push together. We made love like that many times. Sheathed in darkness. Blissful, tender, natural, unaffected. Made for each other we were.

Now he is telling me to forget him. He won't say that he feels more for *her,* simply that he is indebted. He is not conscious of the shadow of satisfaction that twists the corner of his mouth. It is punishment. A senseless show of loyalty to someone he barely knows. He is not for her. He is against me. She will reap what I have sown simply because she was there when I was not. Rage rises in me. It isn't fair. We almost kiss and he runs away. His face, contorted with emotion, slides from my view.

I watch him go. Almost excited because I know I move him still but then, there is an empty space where he has been. A grey street. A fluorescent light. Church and Gerrard. A dingy student hostel. I turn this way, then that. I have no direction and no purpose. I stand. I want him back. To enter stage left. He exited right. Down Church. Uptown. Out of my life. Into my history. I want to scream but I know if I open my mouth that I will fill with air rather than expel it. I walk back inside. Take the elevator to the nineteenth floor and lie down on the little bed. I hold the handmirror above my face.

This is what I see when I lie down. Eyes feline. Liquid green. Skin stretched wide over cheekbones. Eskimo-like in a heat wave. Nose storybookish, pink lips stretched wide over white, even teeth, a little bit crooked no matter what the angle. Slavic. People say it all the time. Hair leonine, thanks to the Portuguese girl on Yonge who spent about an hour on it earlier.

It gave us enough time to bond. From the Azores, cut and pasted into Toronto. Like me an independent city woman, belying rural roots, big family, Catholic, island background. She was dating a Filipino with a great body and a surly mother. They had been together two years, saw each other twice a week and then on Saturdays and Sundays. They never fought. Once you do, you never go back, right? Her questioning eyes met mine briefly in the mirror but certain in her theory she went back to my hair without waiting for an answer. The silver Jesus on a cross glinted around her neck. It had never occurred to me that two people would not fight.

When I see him he says my words are like knives but he loves them too. They make him laugh. They make him hard. He is sticking with her but he won't give my letters back. They are his now. He says that he loves them. She will never write like that for him. I resent the comfort he takes in them. He will have that always. Read. Reread.

What do I have? He offers friendship and alternately I wave it away coolly and bat it away hotly, angrily lashing out at him, standing there. Immovable like the skyscrapers he has grown up with. I am alien. The impostor, the evil one, the storm in the teacup, the upsetter of the applecart. I wonder if I am bad and decide that I am not. I will force myself to pray for him, for her, for them. Instead of hoping it will all go terribly wrong and he will wake up every morning struggling to catch breath, realizing, realizing. Her presence mundane, his debt larger than ever. It will never happen if I hope for it.

I pray, asking the best for him, secretly hoping it will ensure the worst. I am bad. Green eyes glint, long, liquid, almond shaped. Like this, I am goddess. He had been my handmirror many times. Looking down on me, watching as he fucked me, reflecting me, reading me. Sighing when I sighed, pressing murmurs into my hot cheek. He made me like this. Took the girl. Made a woman. Does he not remember? I do. I had changed.

When I returned home, I could no longer press myself back into the Ireland that I had spent a long, harsh winter lovingly projecting onto bleak, blank banks of Canadian sky and snow and concrete. Dislocated, I felt around the edges of my old self and found new angles that hadn't been there before. The bustle of family and friends was dimmed, as if it still had to cross an ocean to reach me. I delighted in the longed-for endless twilights, the fresh grassy scent of the air and the soft, temperate sun, distantly, as though they were pinned behind glass in a museum. Relics of a different life, put out of reach by time and experience. When we had been together in Toronto, I was restless, needing to go back home. When I finally did, I realized that I never could.

I call out from limbo. *Wait!* Tone deliberately muted for a public street, as though he has simply forgotten a book in my hand. He isn't playing. His face contorts as he turns to go. Love? Hate? He says that he is capable of neither. You're evil. Face twists. Turns away. Runs away. Leaving me. Alone. Church and Gerrard.

I light candles and pray. I lie. Alone. Look into the mirror. The city respires noisily. Skin stretches over bone. Bones protrude. He won't say he cares more for her. It's the timing he says. Ours was always lousy. Church and Gerrard. I pray. You're evil. Everywhere skyscrapers point. Alone. I move like a cell in an artery.

I look east. The spit. An oasis. No buildings. Trees and a beaver dam. He took me there once. We raced. We were lovers. I loved him. I want to go back. Go east. Walk back through all the sunrises until I find the one before the spit. Be with him again. He had been mine and I let him go. Told him to fuck off he says. I never I say. Well you didn't stay. Now there's someone else. Can't just tell her to fuck off. But you can tell me to fuck off? He won't say he cares more for her. It's the timing.

Face contorted. Upset, he says. You're evil. We might never see each other again. You never know he says. I'm indebted. You are not—you just don't care. I do but I can't go through this anymore. It's the timing. Ours was always lousy. I want the spit. Me and him. Our bikes. Sticky skin. The smell of the bar. Tender, searching sex in the dark. The gods are against us.

Church and Gerrard. I pray. I light candles. You're evil he said. You're evil. Somewhere a siren sings. Fluorescent light. Grey street. Church and Gerrard. You're evil. His eyes are the colour of the predawn sky. Before the warmth has seeped in. Blue and white and green and yellow. Watercolour strength. Face contorts. You're evil. He slides from my view down Church Street. I lie. Church and Gerrard. Dead heat. Bones protruding. Finally, I close my eyes. And I pray.

Canadian Birds
Yiwei Hu

Bird shit falls on my face and I want to cry, because before this I have always liked pigeons. They look really cute in pictures and on TV, but I guess photographers and moviemakers don't like capturing them scrounging and shitting.

I look around and hope that no one has noticed. My parents are ahead of me, their backs turned; the old men around me are playing Chinese chess on stone tables. I frantically dig in my pockets for a handkerchief.

"Ai lao Zhou-ah! Ni lai kan!"

I jump. I flush when I see that the old men are laughing at me. Spotted fingers are pointing; wooden soldiers are left without direction on their grid-like battlefields. Halted in my search for a handkerchief, I feel a glazed look slide over my face.

My parents must've heard them, because they're also hysterical with laughter. I watch these people contort their faces and wheeze for air. My eyes prickle like crazy, but I won't cry.

"Don't just stand around," Dad finally chokes out. "Get a tissue or something."

"I don't have one."

"Here. Wipe it off." Stepmother, gasping for breath and her face bright red, proffers a tissue.

It's one of those individually wrapped tissues that they give out on airplanes. I read the Chinese characters on it. *Sweet-smelling sanitary paper.* I put it to my nose. It doesn't smell sweet.

"Dongli! Hurry up and wipe it off!"

With that, Stepmother and Dad are gone again. I try to hurry after them, but today I can't wipe and walk at the same time. My limbs simply will not cooperate.

It's probably because I'm tired. My monkey watch tells me it's 10:32 PM in China. Stepmother should've sent me to bed two hours ago, because she says I need to grow. But here, in strange *Duolunduo*, the bright cobalt sky permits no sleep.

I wipe my face roughly. The pigeon shit is slimy against my cheek. Warm and slimy. What an ugly combination. Stupid pigeon, it's all fat and grey. Canadian birds are so disgusting. No bird in China would ever defecate on loyal communist passersby, or the chairman would have them arrested and shot. That's what happens to anti-communist revolutionaries.

I take a good look at the old men, who have resumed their games. Are they capitalist defectors? Is that why they're here, in *Duolunduo*? To escape their deserved punishment?

I want to wave my red necktie at them. The cowards betrayed us to the capitalists. My necktie is red with the blood of loyal soldiers, who died at these murderers' hands. How can they still sit here and play their games and pretend to be Chinese? Traitors. A bunch of no-good traitors.

One of them takes a tissue out of his pocket and noisily blows his nose. A careless flick of his wrinkled wrist, and the scrunched-up tissue lands unceremoniously on the ground.

Sniffing, I fold up the shit-stained tissue in my palm and very deliberately put it back in my pocket. I don't litter. Chairman Mao wants a clean China.

* * *

This morning Stepmother forced me to change the time on my watch to *Duolunduo* time. I had to turn back twelve hours.

But why should we go back in time? This is an evident sign of Chinese superiority. Our civilization is definitely ahead of the times. I cannot understand why these *wai guo ren* here should insist on turning back the wheel of progress.

"Dongli, don't argue," Dad reprimands. "And hurry up. We must go grocery shopping."

Because Mr. Liu's house, where we are temporarily staying, is, according to Stepmother, in the middle of nowhere, we must take the subway to get to a store.

I stroll nonchalantly along the platform. I make sure only to walk in the yellow strip right along the edge. I'm not afraid of the train. I'm not afraid of falling in. Chairman Mao wants his people to be brave. Dad wants me to be brave. So I show them.

A white man is watching me. The capitalist *bai guei* bastard probably thinks that I don't know anything about taking the subway. I'll show him. We Chinese have three cities with full subway systems, while these Canadians only have two.

"Dongli! Step away from the edge!"

Stepmother's bony knuckles rap me on the head. I drift back resentfully.

"*What?* Laogong, why is your daughter looking at me like that?" Her eyes dart to Dad, seeking support, but he averts his gaze. "Dongli, you really want to get killed? You want to get hit by the train?"

"No."

"Then don't walk along the edge. And stop scratching your hair. You look like a monkey with lice. Laogong-ah, maybe your daughter has lice."

"She doesn't." The response is clipped, automatic.

"You never know what dirty habits she picked up from your mother's house."

"Don't bring my mother into this."

"I knew we shouldn't have brought her along—Dongli! Stop fidgeting— see what I mean?"

Dad throws her an impatient glance.

That shuts her up.

Stepmother silently fumes. Her skeletal hands worm into her purse. Out come a cigarette and a lighter. She holds the white stick between her lips and lovingly touches the tip to the flame. I wrinkle my nose. I hate the smell of cigarettes. I pinch my nostrils and watch her puff out smoke like a train engine.

Then an Indian man approaches her. His maroon windbreaker says "TTC" on the sleeve. He says something, and Stepmother flushes. She promptly stomps out her cigarette and fervently repeats something to the Indian. *So-lee? So-lee?* I don't understand what she's saying. Neither does the Indian man. But he seems to be mysteriously satisfied. He leaves.

"What did he say?" I ask.

She glares at me. "He said 'If that child walks along the platform one more time, we'll call the police and have her arrested.'" She snaps her purse shut. "Isn't that right, Laogong?"

Dad doesn't say anything, but I know he heard her. I wish Stepmother would stop talking. He's already annoyed and if she pushes him any more they'll end up having a fight on the subway platform.

"Your daughter is so stubborn. She's bringing trouble on us already. Why don't you—"

"Can you just shut up?" Dad finally snaps. Several people turn to stare. Stepmother grows silent, but taps and taps her fingers; they miss her cigarettes, so they make do with the metal rim of her purse.

"Women, they never know when to shut up."

My cheeks grow warm. I feel like Dad's a big hypocrite. He's always told me that we shouldn't air our dirty laundry in public, so why is he doing this? Does he want everyone to know exactly how dysfunctional we are?

On the other hand, these *wai guo ren* can't even understand what Stepmother and Dad are shouting about.

But I *want* them to understand. I want all this stupid family bickering to be heard and understood. If all they hear from Stepmother and Dad is gibberish to them, won't they just think my parents are idiots? And won't they think that all Chinese people are idiots, too? I don't want them to think I'm dumb.

"I still think you were stupid to bring her," Stepmother restarts after a while. "What can she do? She can do nothing but—"

"I told you that you shouldn't smoke. They don't like it here."

• • •

Yesterday my parents said goodbye to Mr. Liu; they found an apartment.

The apartment is bare, other than the furniture that my parents salvaged from someone's garbage.

"Canadians are so nice," Dad says. "The guy was moving, so he didn't mind giving it all away. If this was in China, he would've charged us at least three hundred yuan. He was nice enough to drive us and the furniture over in his truck too. I offered the *bai guei* thirty dollars, but he just smiled and refused."

I frown. Here we are, barely three days in *Duolunduo,* and my father is already eating out of the capitalists' hand. It's just a couple of chairs and a stupid mattress! And the mattress has a huge yellow stain on it. Big deal.

"Come sit with me, Dongli." He pats the space on the mattress beside him. "It's really comfortable."

I obey. The mattress is soft and bouncy. I can't even feel the springs in it. But still, it smells and looks bad.

Dad offers me a slice of white bread out of a plastic bag. I shake my head. It looks as if it would taste of chalk.

"C'mon. Try it."

I grudgingly take it. I chew a piece. It tastes…good; unfamiliar, but good. So fluffy and white. Is that why capitalists are white? Because they eat so much white bread?

"We should teach her some English," Stepmother says, "before we send her to school."

School?

"Am I going to school after you find a job?" I try very hard to veil my enthusiasm. I don't know why I do that. I didn't use to. But lately it seems to have become a habit.

Stepmother bursts out laughing.

"What? What's so funny?"

"It'll take a while for us to find jobs," Dad explains.

"How long?"

"I don't know. Three months? Six months? A year? Who knows?" He smiles and ruffles my hair.

"But why would it take this long?"

"Because it's very difficult to find a job."

"What your father means is that it's hard to find a job other than washing dishes at a Chinese restaurant."

"But why? Why would it take so long?"

"Because we don't speak English as well as people who were born here."

"And they don't accept our degrees," Stepmother mumbles, a cigarette between her lips.

"Don't smoke in here." Dad waves his hands, clearing smoke from the air.

"Why not?"

"You should quit."

"I'm telling you, I will."

"You always tell me you will, and you never do."

"I'll start tomorrow."

"You always tell me that too."

"So when am I starting school?" I ask, hoping to distract them.

Stepmother throws Dad a contemptuous glance. "Tomorrow," she says.

I bury my excitement in a mouthful of white bread. "How much do we have to pay?"

"Nothing." Stepmother looks at me then looks away. She blows out some smoke. I cough. I look down.

"Let's teach her some English. Repeat after your stepmother."

"Why am *I* teaching her?"

"I'm tired. I need to get some sleep."

"It's just jet lag. You need to get over it. Besides, she's *your* daughter."

"Your pronunciation is better."

She rolls her eyes. "Fine." She takes another drag on her cigarette. Then she smothers it on the ashtray.

"You really should quit. Cigarettes are expensive here."
"I thought I was supposed to be teaching her English."
Pause. Dad opens his mouth and closes it. "Fine."
"My name is Dongli," Stepmother says in an alien voice.
"My name is Dongli," I mimic.
"I live in Toronto."
"I live in Toronto." I pause. I don't want to ask her what that means. Then
I decide that I should, lest she grill me on it later. "*Shen me shi* Toronto-*ah*?"
"Toronto is *Duolunduo* in English."
"Oh."
"I like ay-pple."
"I like ay-pple."

• • •

I'm eating a fried egg sandwich. I made it myself. I made it myself because
yesterday Dad told me I was going to school, and that Stepmother was going
to make me a sandwich, but then Stepmother turned out to have a job
interview at McDonald's so she forgot. Dad was trying to sleep, so he couldn't
help either. I didn't make a mess; that was good, because Stepmother can't
say anything.

But she *would* probably say something about my sitting alone in the
lunchroom. "Why can't you talk to anyone? Are you dumb? How else are
you going to learn English? Laogong-ah, your daughter is stupid."

I'm not. It's just very hard to do as she says. Stomach acid threatens to
flood my mouth. I can't speak a word of English—not entirely true, but what
good are the three sentences that Stepmother taught me, when it comes to
making friends?

Yeah, okay, your name is Dongli. And you live in Toronto—but that much
is obvious, because we *all* live in Toronto. And you like apples. Who cares?

How can I make friends with these *wai guo ren* if I don't speak their
tongue?

This is weird. *Wai guo ren* means "outside nation people." Foreigners.
But that makes no sense. We are the foreigners. We are *wai guo ren*.
I make a note not to use that term again.

It's not that I don't want to make friends. Of course I want friends.
I examine the *hei guei* at a nearby table. His thick, tightly frizzed hair is
cropped closely to his chocolate scalp. He and his *bai guei* friend seem
to be negotiating a trade between cookies and chips.

There are so many words that I have not thought about before. *Hei guei*
means black ghost, and *bai guei* means white ghost.

Neither of them looks very ghostly. I remind myself to purge those words from my vocabulary as well.

How ironic. I'm whittling down my Chinese vocabulary, without expanding its English counterpart. Thus, my overall vocabulary is decreasing. Dumb girl. Stepmother's probably right about me.

I thought that I'd absorb English like a sponge and then just be able to scream it out in some sort of holy language frenzy. But I didn't. I still only know three sentences in English.

My name is Dongli.

I live in Toronto.

I like ay-pple.

The last sentence turns out to be handy—sort of.

Mr. Faber is passing around snacks. I have a choice of a pear or an apple. Happy that I can finally show off some of the English Stepmother taught me, I loudly proclaim "I like ay-pple!"

He frowns. He doesn't understand.

"I like ay-pple," I repeat.

Mr. Faber's bushy *bai guei* eyebrows are bunched up. He looks as if he has a line of fur stuck above his eyes.

A wave of panic tugs at my heart. A slightly off-beat pulse. A surge of red, red blood to my cheeks. I feel hot. A couple of kids snicker.

"*Bu shi* ay-pple. *Shi* ahh-pple," the girl beside me whispers. She's my official interpreter until I learn some basic English.

I blush. "*Xie xie.*"

I turn to Mr. Faber. I'm going to say it right this time. I'll prove that I'm not dumb like they think I am—

But Mr. Faber is gone. He is strolling down the next row. I want to call him back, to show him that I'm smart, but what do I say? Besides, he's raising his unibrow at me. He points at my desk.

Right.

In Toronto you don't have to stand up when you speak with a teacher. In Toronto you don't have to wear the red necktie everyday. In Toronto you don't have to salute the picture of Chairman Mao. But in Toronto you still have to obey the teacher.

I sit down.

He's left me an apple and a pear.

◆ ◆ ◆

Mrs. Grady, my ESL teacher, is taking all her ESL kids to No Frills. We are going to make pizza.

It confused me at first why we would need to make pizza for a class. What could we possibly learn? But I soon saw through Mrs. Grady's pretence of fine cuisine for the vocabulary exercise it really was.

"What do you want on your pizza, Dongli?"

"Peppers."

"Is that all?"

"Everything else other people say already."

Mrs. Grady appears a little concerned about my apathy, but she doesn't press the issue. She herds us inside, fervently pressing a finger to her lips.

It's the first time that I've been in a Canadian supermarket. My parents take me grocery shopping, but we only ever go to Chinatown. The stores there are smelly and dirty. People there speak Cantonese instead of Mandarin. They despise Dad and me for being Mainlanders and only buying food on sale. White people's supermarkets are really different. There is so much light, and so much space! I run down one aisle after another, much to Mrs. Grady's surprise. I must tell Dad and Stepmother about this place. This is so much nicer than shopping at Chinatown—

"Look out! Dongli!"

I slam into pile of boxes. Bottles of barbecue sauce roll everywhere.

I'm really in trouble now; Mrs. Grady won't like me anymore.

But nothing happens. An attendant in a green shirt comes up and quickly restores the bottles to their original configuration. No one yells at anyone. Then Mrs. Grady pays for our groceries and we head back to school.

On the way back, I help Mrs. Grady carry the groceries. She tells me that I'm learning English very quickly, and that I won't need her help for much longer. I want to tell her that I will miss her and her not-so-subtle vocabulary exercises, but I don't say anything. I lose my words. Perhaps I should take her exercises more seriously.

Later Mrs. Grady gives me two slices of leftover pizza to take home. As I walk back to the apartment, I eat my stone cold pizza. My jaw hurts from chewing, so I don't eat the crusts. I rip the crusts to shreds and feed them to pigeons.

Pigeons are not grey all over. Their chest feathers shimmer subtly with colour. Hard to see, but it's there.

• • •

"Why didn't you say you wanted something else on your pizza?" Dad presses.

"Everyone else already said what I wanted to say."

"What about banana? Orange? Ay-pple?"

"Ah-pple."

"What?"

"Nothing. Just that you can't put these things on a pizza."

Stepmother pipes up. "Why not?"

I look at her pityingly. To her, western cuisine will forever be a mystery.

• • •

Two in the morning, and I am wide awake. I can't sleep. My monkey glows brilliantly, showering a fibrous light over my tangled blankets.

When we were packing, they threw out everything Mom had given me. The watch was the only thing that survived their vigilance.

"She's way too old for these things." Stepmother was busy riffling through my closet and smoking with one hand, and stuffing my things into an orange plastic bag with the other. "Laogong-ah, look, your stupid ex-wife bought her a doll. A doll. She's nine, not two. I'm throwing this out."

"Please don't—"

"Don't argue with us, Dongli. Your mother"—*stepmother*— "is absolutely right. You are too old for these toys."

"What about the jigsaw puzzles? I am not too old for those."

"I don't know how a woman can buy jigsaw puzzles for her nine-year-old." Stepmother shook her head, causing the cigarette in her mouth to wobble; the smoke zigzagged. It reminded me of military air shows.

Stepmother stuffed my things into the stretched-open mouth of the plastic bag. I didn't protest. Instead I helped her. We threw out toys and books and frilly dresses. My head felt feverish. My room felt clean.

Later Dad said it was good—a girl my age didn't need any more ideas. Stepmother gave him a strange look.

• • •

What Dad said reminded me of an incident at school.

A few days before we left for Canada, I was in class, learning about Chairman Mao's glorious struggle against the evil capitalists. The boy beside me was fidgeting intensely, his sparse eyebrows knitted together—sort of like Mr. Faber's unibrow. He was bored, impatient, annoyed, what?

His hand shot up in the air.

"What is a capitalist anyway?"

The teacher didn't say anything for a while. In the silence that followed, you could hear the gears in her brain cranking maniacally. Then they seemed to suddenly click into the right configuration and her mouth exploded.

"How stupid. Who doesn't know what a capitalist is? A capitalist is disgusting, vile, greedy—"

"Yeah, but what *is* it? How do we know it's bad, if we don't even know what it is?"

Collective class gasp. Interrupting the teacher? Mr. Faber might not have minded that much, unless you've been really rude already, but in China, you never spoke out of turn.

Our teacher was getting impatient. "I am going to put an end to this silly discussion right now. Listen to me, boys and girls. Chairman Mao says that we must hate and fight capitalism. Capitalists are the essence of evil. And that is enough. You don't need any more ideas."

Was that what Dad meant? That Chairman Mao's ideas were enough for me?

I'm not sure I understand. Should everyone have the same ideas? Chairman Mao's ideas? But at my new school, no one talks about the chairman. And Mr. Faber says that we should all be different.

Maybe it's because Mr. Faber is a capitalist. But he doesn't seem very evil. Then again, perhaps teachers are an exception.

I can't remember what Mao said on the subject.

◆ ◆ ◆

I have finally convinced Stepmother and Dad to shop at white people's stores. I told them that it's a lot less smelly and people are nicer. At first Dad wouldn't believe me, because "true friends are always of your own kind." But Stepmother wanted to give white people's stores a try, because the No Frills near our apartment was much closer than Chinatown.

The first time we shopped there, Stepmother went crazy. She ran down aisle after aisle and pulled in everything and anything. The cart was full of shiny colour.

Dad apparently did not like shiny colour. Stone faced, he removed almost everything that she had chosen. But the mints, in their inconspicuous grey, went unnoticed.

There was no going back. Mints are now a regular on our shopping list. Stepmother has been going through them like crazy. They have been instrumental in helping her quit smoking, she claims.

Dad looks on approvingly as she grabs a large bag of spearmints. She beams, and shows her pearly teeth. They aren't yellow and smelly. At least, not yet.

Dad thinks she's quit, but I know better. She hides her cigarettes and lighter under the mattress, exactly under the big yellow spot, and smokes on the balcony when he goes to work. Her nicotine-yellow nails she covers with nail polish. Then she sucks on a few mints before he comes home, so he'll be none the wiser.

Last night the wristband of my watch broke. The wrinkled leather along the second hole cracked. I wanted to tape it back together, but we don't have any tape. Well, we have tape. But it isn't good tape like we have in school. It's the crappy, slippery kind Dad brought from China.

Mao did say that we shouldn't trust products made by capitalists, but we haven't died yet from using capitalist water and eating capitalist food. Maybe Mao was right, but he was right in another country, another time.

I left my broken watch on the kitchen counter, thinking that I would get some tape later. But this morning I couldn't find it. It isn't where I left it.

"Dad, have you—" Never mind, Dad's out job hunting. Besides, he hates it when I lose things and always gets angry.

I can't ask Stepmother either, because she's always in a bad mood and she also hates it when I lose things.

Why do I have to be so stupid? In a state of barely suppressed panic I rip open cupboards and pull out drawers. Where is it? Where could it have gone?

In my haste my hand tips over a glass of water. The water flattens, invades the counter space and waterfalls off the edge. The glass rolls; my hand moves to catch it but I'm too slow and too late. It falls and shatters. The noise is awful.

"What happened?"

Stepmother is standing with her arms crossed, sucking on a mint. I stare at her.

"I asked you a question. What were you doing, slamming drawers like that?" Silence. "Answer me!"

"I was looking for something."

She sucks hard on the mint; it makes a curious sound, like a very loud cricket. The freshening smell is almost as bad as cigarette smoke. "What are you looking for?"

I hesitate. Her face creases in anger and I shudder. "My watch."

"So you lost it."

"No I didn't. I know it's somewhere in the apartment."

"Sounds to me like you lost it."

"I just misplaced it, that's all."

"How many times do I have to tell you to be careful with things? Why can't you just—you really think I like being here with you?"

I am stunned. I don't know what to say. Why is she asking me this? What does she want to hear? What does she want me to say?

She opens her mouth, but she falls silent. Her gaunt body sags, forcing itself into a chair. She hides behind her veil of long black hair. Not a sound comes out of her; only quivers and water.

There is something about all this that I just don't understand. The fluidity of it makes my legs wobbly like plastic jugs full of water. I walk over to Stepmother and put my arms around her. Weakly she tries to break through my hold. I hang on obstinately and I don't know why. She cries harder, but she no longer pushes me away. Instead she latches onto my arms, her head resting on my shoulder.

"It's okay," I whisper. "We'll be fine."

She shakes her head. She mumbles words, but I can't hear them. Eventually she detaches herself from me and fishes something out of the garbage.

She avoids my eyes as she hands it to me. She must think I'm mad at her. I'm not. My monkey is okay; he's laughing and ticking.

When she turns to leave I grab her hand. She hugs me close; her bony arms dig into my ribs. It hurts, but it's a good hurt. I want to cry, but I can't. I guess it's okay, because I have lots of time to learn.

I let go of Stepmother. I tell her that I'll be back. I come back with cigarettes, her lighter, and toilet paper for her nose. She starts to laugh. Snot spews everywhere. She laughs even more, and struggles to clean her face.

"You little devil, how'd you know they were there? No wonder you always look at me like that when we buy mints." Suddenly she's scared. "Does your father know?"

I giggle. "No, of course not."

"No, of course not." She smiles. "Come with me. I need a smoke." She spits her mint into the garbage. "I never liked mints anyway."

We step onto the balcony. The air feels nice and clean—now, but Stepmother is already lighting up. Grey tendrils spiral upward. She blows smoke rings. Stepmother is making her mark on the atmosphere.

"I'll buy you some tape," she says.

I look at her. "It doesn't matter. You don't need to. We have tape."

"It's not very good."

Above our heads I hear murmured shouting; something about smokers, I think. A window slams.

Stepmother says she'll quit tomorrow. Then we both burst out laughing. A pigeon flutters by. I wave.

Poems
Naya Valdellon

RETURN TO SENDER

Was she thinking: grief
is a letter you mail to yourself

once the turnstile's been turned
at the subway station

x number of times. The delay
is necessary, chosen in advance

for a day like this, when she pushes
the door open into a room

made immaculate, and relatives
made inquisitive, by an infant's

early death. The father exhales
facts, one at a time: heart failure.

Two days of life. Less than one hour
for the cremation. The periods

like steel bolts clicking into place.
She hears the footsteps of a man

who hands the ashes back
in a white envelope to the mother

who accepts it with the calm
of a commuter holding a token

to a train ride that will carry her
further and further from the right address.

FROM "FIRST WINTER PASSING"

1. Daylight Saving Time

Thirteen hours between Toronto and Manila—
The hands of the clocks in my room ache to be moved—

Dali's watches wilt in the waning light, in the poster
above my head. I am outside the frame. I count.

Tell me, what's another hour to lose while we loosen
our tongues, stifle yawns? A fly grazes the sagging face

above our faces. Ants kiss on top of the pocket watch.
Here and now, the cliffs between us persist.

2. Question and Answer

Tell me about your country.

A constellation of islands
near the world's waistband.

Tell me what it looks like.

A crouching old woman
with a walking stick
and a hand on her hip.

I don't mean on a map.

You mean from a plane?
Through window panes? A mirror?
Describing seven thousand selves
in one sentence is impossible.

I'm not asking for it.

No, you're better at imperatives.

4.

Silver white winters that melt into springs—
not my song, not my seasons. In my country,
summer is warming up, doing morning stretches.

Here, his fingers skate on my skin. My blood hisses
as I parse his vocabulary of sighs. He tries hard
to say the word *mahal*, which means both love

and expensive. His tongue teeters over *kita*,
a possessive pronoun roping You to Me, as well
as the interrogative "See?" I want him to stumble

his way into my archipelago. Later, our breaths
interlace in the frosty air. The spectres
of our unsaid things look white and willful.

5.

News from Manila   My father's had a stroke   Of bad luck
Bad blood   Blood clot stalling   Traffic in his brain
I should have called   Long distance   When I dreamt of him
Playing Chopin's *Heroic Polonaise*   Last song over Warsaw radio
Before the slaughter   Why do I know this   My father loved
The piano   Loves   My poems   Ways of passing time
My lover brews espresso to keep me going   He broke up with his girlfriend
Does the taste of her persist   *Fall back*   I will be patient
Under observation   Hospitals skew hours   My father gets impatient
When his fingers press the wrong keys   Ice plummeting
From the CN Tower   Keeps us indoors   He has no key yet
Miles between us   *Arpeggios*   Chords like a phone ringing
My mother's voice   Metallic and rusty   With relief
Wheeled to a private room   *Spring forward*   This is good
Can't stand up on his own   Yet   Holding my hand in his sleep

6.

I am writing him a letter, a catalogue
of streets, slushy with the voices of loonies.
I wonder whose children they could be,
whose lovers.

Santa Claus squats on the corner
of Bathurst and Bloor, unable to return north
to December. He scratches his beard,
holds up a sign: *Sleigh broke down.*
Passersby who throw him coins pay tribute
to their childhoods.
It's my birthday,
the man on St. Clair declares, as if it were
a demand, palms turned up like a saint
that's strolled out of church and misplaced
his halo, lips parted for what could be kisses,
what could be curses.

A woman on Bloor, her back to the Future
Bakery screams, *The fucking lights don't change!*
The lights—
Across her, the white man
glows, the outline of his body telling pedestrians
to go.
Take out the trash, mutters the man
on College Street who dives into blue boxes
for wine bottles. He sidesteps the man
on a unicycle who pedals past everyone
with his hands outstretched, asking for nothing
but snow, embracing this city of grids and signs.

P.S. It's impossible to get lost here,
yet impossible for some of us to find our way.

AT THE TRAVEL AGENCY, I FIND

myself parcelling thoughts into paragraphs
to be mailed, as if he had already left.

One: after three flights of stairs,
how could he have guessed which
was the right room, there being no sign
on the door?
                    Two: his sense of direction
has nothing to do with the compass-
shaped lighter in his pocket, yet another
contrivance.
                    Three: white squares
on walls where maps must have hung,
tour brochures still on monobloc chairs,
steel cabinets perched on trolleys,
all make up one story: even this place
is in the process of moving.
                    (A travelling
travel agency, like a garage sale
in a real garage.)
                    I think of a neighbour
who parked her car out on the curb
while strangers rifled through silverware
and books, furniture and shirts: a houseful
of detritus in the driveway, selling for less
than their worth.
                    She looked on with resolve
(or was it nonchalance?), her eyes saying:
No room for baggage; I am bartering
my heart for another life.
                    And now he—
who is neither neighbour nor stranger to me—
what would he say in this, my story
of the last errand?

(That he has been
a tourist all this time? That his hunger
for border jumping is insatiable?)
                              I sit on the edge
of my chair, waiting for—there it flickers,
as an agent hands him his plane ticket—
the look of a child asking if it is all right
to leave, as if permission were mine to give.
                    I watch the agent reading,
taking forever to turn the page. I want to ask
where the maps are, to see the red dots—
like the lit ends of cigarettes—in place
of the cities we love.
                              Instead, I make my knuckles
crack a code into the air: *Leave already,*
so you can write to me. I need
to read your version of this story.

The Iron Curtain
Sabrina Ramnanan

"Neil, what you studying in school, boy? Interracial marriages?" my mom asked.

"International relations," I said. Suddenly I was slurping down the rest of my coffee in a rush to get out.

She turned to my father. "I send he to 'U.F.T.' to study international relations but I feel he studying interracial marriages. I does see we son knocking about with a little girl of the…*Asian persuasion*." She glowered over her mug at me, and I back at her. "I getting a Chinese girl for my daughter-in-law," she said. "Allyou think she could cook a roti?"

She did this to stir my dad and it worked every time.

"She go feed me chow mein and pork till I dead," Dad said. "Noodles, noodles, noodles! My backside already thin like a noodles. How I could survive on that?" He waved his bony arms.

"Don't forget fortune cookies." My mother sipped the last drop of *Milo* from her mug and headed to the family room.

My dad followed her. "Me ain't want no cookie with fortune inside. I done know my fortune if my son marry a Chinese girl: I go dead from eating noodles."

My girlfriend was from the Philippines. She had almond-shaped eyes and hair like black silk. I really began to notice her when she started sitting next to me in a political science class. She would stare intently at the professor and scribble furiously into her notebook. When we began sharing notes, it amazed me how she still managed to underline all her headings with a glittery pink pen. Every *i* was dotted, every *t* crossed, every lower case *y* finished with an elaborate flourish. Her fixation on a perfect grade point average fascinated me too, but it was Rosi's determination to get what she wanted that really attracted me.

"You ain't go dead from eating noodles alone, Satish, SARS go surely speed up the process," Mom said, rearranging the pillows on her recliner.

When she knew she'd vexed my father into a huff, my tiny mother would slip on her fuzzy orange slippers and climb up into her leather recliner. She'd close her eyes, a satisfied smile stretching across her thin lips, until his ludicrous notions had lulled her off to sleep. I always wondered what sort of dreams she had, falling asleep this way.

I didn't understand then what the big deal about Rosi was. I hadn't once said I wanted to marry her. The truth was, I hadn't even thought about it until Dad made it his business to point out what a big mistake marrying her would be. After that, Rosi became a big part of my life.

The first time I brought her home Dad was sitting at the kitchen table, shelling pistachios and wearing a surgeon's mask. Rosi stiffened. I was mortified. We watched him line the shells up in neat little rows like missiles ready to fire. I imagined the smug expression he wore beneath his protective mask. I knew he was daring me to introduce him to Rosi, so I did. And for good measure I said, "Isn't she something?"

Smiling bravely, Rosi stepped forward, her small, bronzed hand in mid extension. But when Dad's only acknowledgement was a nod and a grunt before turning back to his pistachios, I caught Rosi swiftly by the elbow and, slipping an arm around her waist, marched my mystified girlfriend down into the basement, away from the enemy and the cracking of shells.

Rosi abandoned me at the bottom of the steps to explore my basement apartment on her own. I trailed after her in awkward silence, trying to piece together an apology on my father's behalf. But she paid me no attention as she scanned my bookshelf for interesting titles and gazed thoughtfully at photographs on the wall. Her composure unnerved me. When she discovered the bar in the far corner, Rosi slid behind the marble countertop and placed two glasses in front of her. "What'll it be?" she said. Her face betrayed no emotion.

"Uh...scotch for me." I paused. "Listen, Rosi, I'm sorry about the way my dad treated you—"

"It's an acquired taste, isn't it? How do *you* like it?" She motioned for me to sit at my own bar, a bottle of Chivas Regal in her hand.

"What?"

"Your drink. How do you like it?"

"Oh. Neat." I licked my lips. "His behaviour was unacceptable and I just want you to know that I'm positive you and I are—"

"On the rocks for me."

"—good for each other."

"A toast?"

"My parents may be wary about interracial dating but that doesn't change the way I feel about you."

"Cheers!"

I sighed, raising my glass to hers. "Did you hear anything I just said?"

Rosi took a sip of her drink. "Every word," she said. "But I have just one question." I watched her swirl the ice cubes around in her amber drink, a mischievous smile playing on her lips.

"Anything."

She leaned across the bar. "Does he know he can't eat pistachios with a surgeon's mask on?"

I laughed, relieved and, leaning forward, I kissed my girlfriend on the mouth for the first time.

When the holidays rolled around two months later I began to see more of my extended family. Mom's older brother, Uncle Adesh, threw the first party of the season and his wife, Auntie Patsy, asked the one question I didn't want to hear: "So, Neil, when you getting married, boy?"

I saw Dad's body go rigid. He clinked the ice cubes in his glass, irritated. "Neil, you ain't introduce Auntie Patsy to your sweetheart yet?" He took a gulp of his drink, eyeing me from over the rim of the glass.

"She's in the powder room, but I'll—"

"Powder room!" My mother snorted. It sounded like *pow-dah* room when she said it. "Where you pick up such hoity-toity lingo from, child?"

Before I could reply something swooped down into the seat beside me. "What she name? What she look like?" I'd never seen Grandpa move so fast. His sharp, old eyes roamed the room for a new, young face.

My cousin Rani, thrice removed, was next to him before I could answer. "How you could keep a secret like this from me, Neil?"

Her husband, whose name I still can't recall, shooed her away and took her spot. "Give the boy some room, " he said. He poured a shot and a half more of rum into my glass and a dash of Coke for colour. "This is man talk."

But Rosi's sudden appearance in the kitchen prevented any kind of talk— man or otherwise—for a few moments. Heads swivelled, necks craned and bodies leaned in all directions to get an unobstructed view of my girlfriend. Rosi looked stunning in her purple satin dress and sweeps of lavender eye shadow across her slanted eyes. Even I stared. She laughed at the awkwardness of the situation, warm and earnest.

"Hi everyone, I'm Rosi," she said with a little wave. As I was wading through the bodies to take her hand and introduce her more formally a distant uncle shouted out: "Patsy, you ain't see Neil's girlfriend come? Fix she a plate, nuh." I exhaled.

As the room hummed with an excited new energy, Auntie Patsy bustled forward, fanning herself anxiously. She greeted Rosi sincerely but I noticed her fidgeting uncomfortably with the hem of her blouse. Perspiration glistened on her upper lip. I watched her eyes shift from the food on the stove to Rosi and then back again, apologetically.

"What's wrong, Auntie?" I asked.

Her eyes welled with tears. "The food hot like a donkey's backside!" She clutched her bosom. "How this gyal could eat my food?" Rosi and I hid our smiles. "Everyone go say I is a bad hostess if I don't feed she"—she nodded towards Rosi—"but if she eat, the pepper go kill she!"

But Rosi survived Auntie Patsy's cooking and even indulged her by having seconds, which had my auntie beaming for half the night. And while Rosi ate, Grandpa talked. "You like tomatoes?" Rosi nodded. "How about ocro and *aloo*?" She looked confused, but nodded anyway. Grandpa was encouraged. "Pumpkin? Thyme? Onions?" Yes, Rosi liked them all. Grandpa leaned closer to Rosi and lowered his voice. "I inviting you to a exclusive tour of my garden. My thumb green-green!" He winked at her and wiggled his thumb in the air like a crazy hitchhiker.

Rosi raised her glass to Grandpa's, businesslike. "It's a date," she said.

Mom watched the exchange purse-lipped from across the table as she folded a Christmas napkin into little squares, deepening each crease with a belligerent sweep of her trigger finger.

"Neil," she said, "you ain't tell anyone how you do on your midterms."

I sighed. I knew it was a prompt for my father, who chimed in right on cue.

"You nearly failed three exams, ain't that so, Neil?" he paused to empty his glass. "Too much Ring around the Rosi if you ask me." He was drunk.

My uncles and aunties laughed. They didn't understand our cold war. I believe they actually thought it was cute, that I was some kind of lovesick puppy.

"Actually," I said, turning to Uncle Adesh, who was filling thirteen shot glasses right to the brim, "Rosi aced all of hers. Since we've been together, she's reached the top of the class." I winked at her. I was trying to help her, trying to prevent rumours of Rosi's bad influence causing me to flounder in school. It backfired on me though.

"So allyou fall in love and now she smart and you's a duncy-head fool?" Uncle Belly slapped me on the back. Rosi squeezed my hand beneath the table.

"Like the girl do obeah on you or what, Neil?" My mother said, propping her chin on her palm.

Rosi looked quizzically at my mother. "I've never dabbled in mysticism," she said. "Obeah's roots are grounded in African soil and practised in the Caribbean. It's a far way from the Philippines."

A second of stillness silenced the buzz in the room, a wonderful second of awe, until Uncle Belly hooted and slapped the table excitedly. "The girl smart in truth!" He leaned toward my mother, a foolish grin on his round face, "I bet you think the gyal didn't know what obeah is, eh?" My mother glared at him furiously.

"Sound like May Lee to me," Uncle Belly said, nudging my father playfully before emptying a handful of cashews into his huge jowls. "The coconut don't fall far from the tree, man." Adesh and a few other uncles and aunties snickered and exchanged knowing glances.

A shadow of pain swept across my father's brown face. He looked uncomfortable for a moment, unlike the proud man I'd always known. But before anyone else could notice, it was gone and he was slapping a deck of cards on the table saying: "All-Fours. Who's in?"

The next weekend, Rosi came over to watch a movie. We disappeared into the basement again to avoid my father's disapproving grunts and the sour scowl my mother had been sporting since Uncle Adesh's party.

Rosi was unusually somber that evening. She stared unseeingly at the television, back erect, arms crossed. "Are they going to get over this?"

She caught me off guard. She had a way of doing that. "Probably not."

"And you're okay with that." It was statement, not a question, and that made me uncomfortable.

"They're my parents. What choice do I have?" Once I'd said it, I knew it was the wrong thing to say. There was silence for a few moments. Heavy, unforgiving silence.

"Your mother has dismissed me as a sorceress of black magic. Your father refuses to acknowledge my presence. And you're okay with that." Rosi was up from her seat now, pacing slowly in measured steps, her hands clasped behind her back.

"You know that isn't true, and I was just as much a victim of their criticism as you were."

She stopped pacing. "So that makes it okay?"

"Of course not. I'm just saying."

"All you're really saying is that they have licence to insult us because they're your parents."

I looked away. Is that what I was saying? I sat there in the dark, the movie playing in the background, and I wondered if this is how it would end. "I won't let them drive us apart. I say we boycott the rest of the holiday festivities. We'll make a statement," I said, taking her hand and coaxing her down onto the couch again. I'll call Uncle Belly and—"

She shook her head vehemently. "Definitely not." I was taken aback by her conviction. "That's exactly what they want. I want to go."

When she turned her attention back to the movie I pulled her close because I could feel her drifting away. It didn't help and I knew why: she wasn't the problem.

That evening, when Rosi left, I joined my parents in the family room. They were watching a *60 Minutes* special on one man's ability to withstand subzero temperatures without protective clothing. During a commercial, Mom kicked her footrest out on the recliner. "I wonder what kind of girl does visit a boy in the basement of he house?" She picked a piece of lint off the blanket draped across her knees.

"A girl with no *brought-up-sy*," Dad said.

"You think she parents know she does come here and make nest in we basement for hours?"

I watched the reflection of television dance over my parents' dour faces in disbelief. They never even looked at me. "She has feelings," I said to them. "You're driving her away." It came out more desperate than I meant it to. Dad gave me a peculiar look, almost sympathetic, before he rearranged his bones into a more comfortable position from which he didn't have to look at me.

Mom feigned offence. "How that could be, Neil? We haven't said a word to she."

I glared at her. "That's exactly it, Mom. You—," but she held up her hand then. The *60 Minutes* clock was ticking away on the television again. My time was up, our conversation over.

When Uncle Belly threw his annual Christmas Eve party four days later, I showed up with Rosi on my arm. My parents pretended she wasn't there but everyone else welcomed her affectionately. I caught a glimpse of my mother glowering in a dark corner. My father had moved to the other side of the room.

"Lamppost reach! Lamppost reach! Allyou could start the party. I reach."

I turned to see my Uncle Lamppost walking through the front door, the last of my mom's brothers. He towered above us all on his lanky legs. I watched him stoop to kiss the ladies and offer a bejewelled handshake to the men. He had poured every male cousin their first drink, lit their first cigarette behind the shed in his backyard and described to us a woman's anatomy long before we had our first girlfriends. We didn't see him often, so when Uncle Lamppost made his entrance at the Christmas Eve party, the music was turned down and the party gravitated toward him.

"Lamppost, this is Neil's *daahhllingg*," Auntie Patsy cooed, ushering Rosi toward my uncle. Liquor had thickened her accent nicely.

Everyone watched Rosi and Lamppost lock eyes. Lamppost didn't say anything at first; he just stared at Rosi in a bizarre way that made us all a little uncomfortable. He placed his ringed forefinger beneath Rosi's chin and tilted it slightly so that he could see her eyes better. What he said next came out in a whisper, "May Lee."

Uncle Belly erupted into laughter, relieved his eccentric brother hadn't embarrassed him. "I say the same thing myself just the other day, Lamppost! The very same thing."

None of the cousins seemed to know what they were talking about but a familiar titter of gossip washed over the aunties and uncles like blue-green sea foam over rocks at Maracas Beach.

"Who is May Lee, Uncle?" I asked.

Out of the corner of my eye I saw my mother elbowing her way through the crowd toward us. Her black eyes were slits. Her mouth was the very shape of disgust, full of curdled milk, it seemed.

"You father never tell you about May Lee, boy?" Uncle Lamppost laughed, looking around for my dad. I spotted him first. He was sitting in the same corner, downing a scotch on the rocks and looking more morose than ever.

"Satish, what happen to you? Your mouth sew up?" Uncle Lamppost took Rosi by the hand and led her to the sofa, bidding me follow. He accepted a drink from Auntie Patsy, who was trying to squeeze her hips in between Rosi and me. My other relatives stood about in their own circles pretending to make small talk but they were all really straining to catch bits of our conversation.

"May Lee was your father's first love, boy." He turned to Rosi. "And she was as beautiful as you are."

Mom had finally forced her way to the centre of the action. She glared up at Lamppost with her clenched fists set firmly on her waist. "What nonsense you talking, Lamppost!"

Lamppost flashed his dazzling smile and stooped to plant a kiss on his furious sister's cheek before continuing. He would not be outshone by my mother. "This was back in Trinidad, of course." Nostalgia crept into his eyes. "May Lee's father owned the only dry cleaner shop in San Juan in those days. Your father used to drip dhal on his good-good shirts so he could take them to May Lee to wash."

"Your father is a damn fool who does still drip dhal on his good-good shirts," Mom said to me.

I stole a glance at Dad. He had risen from his chair and he looked fearful now.

"So what happened to May Lee?" I asked.

"Your mother. People used to joke she must have really do some good obeah on he backside because just like that"—he snapped his glittering fingers—"your father stopped visiting the cleaners and your parents got married."

My mother scowled deeply. "People in Trinidad does drink too much rum and talk too much stupidness." She sucked her teeth long and hard. "I didn't have to work no obeah on Satish. He know a good woman when he see one," she said, raising her chin.

Uncle Lamppost grinned, his gold tooth glimmering. "I thought you said Satish is a damn fool."

Mom was perspiring at the temples. I admit I enjoyed watching Lamppost exasperate her that way. But I was still confused. "So where did May Lee go?"

Mom turned on me then. Beneath the ire in her eyes I thought I detected a warning to back off. "Boy, hush. You too fast for your own good."

Uncle Lamppost furrowed his brow in thought. "She moved to Tobago around the same time your mother met your father."

"So you drove May Lee away, too," I said to my mom.

My mother's face reddened then. I heard Rosi's sharp intake of breath and suddenly I was aware that my entire family had given up the charade of small talk and were just plain staring now. My mother stood at the centre of it all, and as her gaze fell on Rosi and me it hardened in such contempt that I was chilled to my very core.

She took a step toward me. Her voice trembled when she spoke. "You think May Lee's family would have give their daughter to a coolie like he?" She nodded her head in my father's direction, staggering toward us now.

"Who you calling a coolie, Drupatee?" He never called my mother by her first name. It was always *dear*. "You see me working on a plantation? I am no coolie. In fact, if I is a coolie, then you is one too!"

My mom looked right through him; she wasn't interested in anything he had to say. It dawned on me too, that she knew he was merely trying to derail the present quarrel, or at least, redirect its course. She raged on.

"You think May Lee could have wash and cook and clean for you father? You think she could have manage to cut cane in that hot sun with that child in she belly?" My mother spat the last part out. "I save he!" She stomped her foot. "While that hot little thing abandon your father's bony backside to have she mix-up child in Tobago, I save he!"

Auntie Patsy's meaty hand flew to her chest with a gasp. Uncle Belly was wringing his hands in a corner; his party was ruined. Even Uncle Lamppost had nothing charming to say, so he made a sad attempt to calm my seething mother. The rest of my family murmured amongst themselves and stole furtive glances at my dad. He stood there, a scandalized, angular mess, knowing neither what to say or do.

"And you," Mom whirled on Rosi now, "you, show up here and seduce *my* son with your exotic-erotic magic to repeat history—"

"Enough!" I bellowed it from somewhere deep inside me, the dark place where I'd been burying my resentment. My head spun. Silence pregnant with anticipation fell over the room and I realized that I would never again have such an opportunity to speak my mind. "Don't say anything else. Not a word," I said. "I'm tired of the backhanded insults, the incessant sarcasm and your flippant attitude toward Rosi." Mom opened her mouth to speak but for the first time in my life I beat her to it. "Have I shamed you in bringing her here, this intelligent, exotic-erotic goddess?" Mom flinched at the sting of my words.

I felt my dad's skeletal hand press into my shoulder, but I shrugged it off boldly.

"No, leave him, Satish!" she said to my father. "We son is a big man now. He could tell off he mother in front of people." And with a sweeping gesture of her arm, she addressed the tense room. "How I could feel shame? No. I is proud-proud right now." The grate of her scorn on my ears infuriated me. She slithered to my dad's side. "And you should be proud too! Look how we son is following in your footsteps, so cozy with Rosi!"

I understood now that she had been holding this against him for their entire marriage. My dad lowered his head under the weight of his guilt and shame and my mom raised hers in unwarranted pride. They stood like imbalanced scales on Judgement Day. I loathed them both at that moment.

"You've had thirty-two years to come to terms with your choices—and they were *your* choices," I said. "Rosi and I are staying together"—I reached for her hand—"She's my girlfriend, not your scapegoat." The colours of embarrassment glowed on my mother's cheeks.

I made to walk away, but Rosi didn't move. She had watched the drama unfold like a spectator and now she was ready to step into her own story, to speak her own parts. She released my clammy hand and moved closely to my parents. "Look at me," Rosi said. "Look very carefully at me." Her composure was more powerful than all the wrath, cynicism or shame that lingered in the air. We hung on to her whispery words. "My name is Rosi Bautista, not May Lee. I'm from the Philippines, not Trinidad. I'm in love with your son—wait, no, don't look away—but it's okay…It's okay because I'm not May Lee."

We all stood in awe of her tenderness. Mom sucked her teeth half-heartedly and then, exhausted by her own resentment, leaned against Dad's bones and allowed herself to weep quietly.

As the action of our drama ebbed, the room grew lively with voices again. "Eh, allyou dry up your tears, nuh. Christmas reach," Uncle Belly said. The circle around us broke apart into smaller groups and we were lost in the renewed merriment and laughter of the party. Uncle Lamppost sauntered over. "I been to plenty-plenty fete in my life, but I never see entertainment like this before. You really steal the show tonight, Drupatee." He pinched her wet cheek, chuckling; she was too drained to respond

My parents looked at Rosi and me. It was too much to expect an apology then—they were still licking their own wounds—so I mumbled: "Half-sister or half-brother?"

Dad shrugged, his eyes glittering with regret. "I never knew," he said.

When Rosi and I snuck out a half hour later, snowflakes were drifting lazily from the night sky. We made fresh prints on the driveway, she and I, hand in hand.

"I'm sorry things turned out the way they did," Rosi said into the darkness. Her hot breath escaped into the frigid night in clouds. "But things look promising, don't they?" She didn't pause long enough for me to answer. "I mean, there is definitely potential for a better relationship between you—us—them—all of us—you know what I mean."

I gave her a peculiar look but she rattled on, puffs of breath dancing from her lips like smoke from a steam engine.

"And I think you were brave, standing up to your mom that way. Thanks for defending me, too. Oh, and I meant everything I said tonight, you know. And isn't it interesting that—"

"Rosi." I stopped walking and took her face in my gloved hands. "I love you, too."

She looked up at me with such coyness, I was taken aback. I smiled. She had a way of doing that.

Safari
Anar Ali

Sultan Uncle placed several glossy brochures in front of Arif and Meena. "I recommend this one." He tapped the brochure for the Tree Tops Lodge & Resort. "Top class luxury. It will be the ultimate safari. Of course you can also try the Serena. Can't go wrong there either. After all the Imam owns that one."

Arif rubbed his goatee as he reviewed the brochures. The hotels weren't exactly what he had in mind. "Actually, Cha-cha, I think Shakeel would enjoy a camping safari more." He turned to his son, who was slumped on a chair behind them, playing with his Game Boy. "What do you say, buddy?" Arif pointed to a poster behind Sultan Uncle's desk. The poster showed a group of white campers, hair rustled, unshaven, sitting around a fire and holding out bottles of beer to the camera. A Masai man stood in the background, wearing a warrior's shield and holding a spear. The sign above the campers read "Discover Kenya in Livingston's Footsteps."

"Yeah, Dad," Shakeel said as he pushed up his glasses. "That would be cool."

"Oh-ho, don't be so foolish." Sultan Uncle scratched his thick belly between two buttonholes. "Those packages are meant for the Europeans only. You know how they are. So much money and still they want to sleep on the ground. What all is the point of being uncomfortable if you don't have to? Doesn't make any bloody sense. Besides, what the hell do you think your father would say if he heard? He would kill me only. No, absolutely not. You are my guests and I will not allow you to live like paupers. Am I right, Meena, or what?"

Meena nodded as she tucked her tortoiseshell sunglasses into a case that hung around her neck. "We don't even camp in Canada, so why would we camp here?"

Meena had not wanted to come to Kenya for a vacation. She would have rather gone to one of their usual vacations spots—Cuba, Jamaica or Mexico, where they stayed at all-inclusive resorts, which provided all their meals and also provided activities to occupy Shakeel.

"It isn't safe there," Meena had said to Arif. Both Arif and Meena's parents agreed. "Don't be ridiculous," Arif's father had said. "Things aren't the way the used to be." They all told him told him countless stories about daylight robberies and carjackings. "I'm telling, these *golas*, they are waiting, waiting for any chance to rob you, to do God knows what else. Why take such unnecessary risks? Especially with Shakeel. Why do you think they call it Nairobbery, hanh?"

But Arif insisted. Going to Kenya would be an adventure. Not only would they go on safari, but it would also be a great way for Shakeel to better understand his roots. "Well, they're not my roots. I was born in England." Meena said. "And in case you've forgotten, your son was born in Toronto."

Meena's parents were from Zanzibar and were studying in England when they met. Their families forced them to marry when Meena's mother fell pregnant with her. They stayed in England until the recession in the 1980s prompted them to emigrate to Canada. Meena found the transition from London to Toronto almost impossible. She missed her friends and couldn't stand the weather. But then she met Arif at university and things changed. Suddenly, she had a full life—filled with friends and activities. Soon after they were married, they opened a dental practice in Fairview Mall at Sheppard Avenue and Don Mills. Arif was a dentist and Meena a hygienist. The practice grew quickly so that before the end of their second anniversary, they opened additional office, this one in Parkway Mall, only ten minutes away at Ellesmere Road and Victoria Park.

Their workload increased significantly—both of them working daily from seven in the morning until nine in the evening on weekdays and nine to five on weekends. They often ate their meals at one of the many restaurants in the food court, some of which were owned by other Ismailis, who generously offered them discounted prices. (Arif and Meena obviously returned the favour—offering excellent rates to these businesses for their families' dental care.) It was tiring, but they both agreed it was the only way to build a business, to build equity and get ahead. Long term, it would pay off.

But after taking maternity leave, Meena decided to quit. Arif encouraged her to come back to work. Don't waste your education, he told her. But

Meena refused. She found it all too overwhelming. Soon after Shakeel's birth, they had been appointed Regular Mukhi-Sahib and Mukhiana-Ma at the Unionville Jamatkhana. Besides working every day, they were now required to lead the ceremonies at the prayer hall each evening, not to mention the many meetings and dinners they also had to attend. Meena had wanted to say no to the appointment—there was hardly any time for anything else as it was. But in the end, she knew that they had no choice. She had never heard of anyone refusing an appointment. Besides, it was an honour and privilege to serve the jamat, and not everyone in the community was given the same opportunity.

Sultan Uncle shoved a tray of samosas leaking grease, fried *mogo* and green chutney toward them. "Come on, eat some more. You know how I don't like such formalities."

Arif took a samosa. Meena refused. "No thanks," she said.

She had signed up for Weight Watchers a few months ago after Munir, the husband of a friend, had joked during a group excursion to the water park at Ontario Place that she still hadn't lost her baby fat. "Don't get me wrong, Meena. I love 'em young." Munir winked and then sprayed her with his water gun. The Weight Watchers guidebook did not list samosas and Meena had no idea how many points one was worth. (Three like a bagel or eleven like a latke?) She certainly did not want to take any chances.

"Take one, *sey*," Sultan Uncle urged Meena. "Just because you are such big-big people living in Canada now doesn't mean you have to be so skinny. Eat, eat, and I'll send you looking nice and healthy. Just like me."

Meena relented and took one, but she only nibbled at it.

"Good girl," he said and then turned to Arif. "I'm telling you, these days things have gotten worse and worse only. You have to be extra careful. These stupid *golas* are looking for a chance. Any bloody chance to rob you, to do God knows what else. Last week only a gang of them robbed Badru Popat. In broad daylight! No shame, I swear. Not only did they take his money, but they beat him senseless and then they stripped the old man of all his clothes. Dear God, what has this world come to? Poor man had to walk home looking like a Masai—holding only *The Kenya Standard* for cover. A picture of President Moi covering his backside and a picture of Kimathi covering his you-know-what. How bloody embarrassing."

Arif shook his head and laughed. "You make it sound worse than an American ghetto."

"It is. Believe you me, it is. And at least in America, you can call dial 911 and the police are there *mara-moja*. But here? The police themselves are corrupt bastards. Don't trust anyone, that is for sure."

"I'm sure we'll be fine. People travel here all the time, without any problems at all."

"All it takes is one problem," Sultan Uncle said.

"I really want Shakeel to have a once in a lifetime experience. Kids learn by doing. It will be like an educational adventure."

Education was a top priority for Arif. They can take many things away from you, he would say to Shakeel, quoting the Imam, but no one can take away your education. For Arif, there was a lesson in everything. Every problem could be turned into an opportunity. Despite his busy schedule, Arif was fully involved in his son's life: he tutored Shakeel daily, helping him patiently with his homework; he attended his hockey games, drove him to his elocution classes. Arif encouraged his son to push himself to the next level in everything he did. They even had a weekly games night; their family room was stacked with games like Trivial Pursuit and Jeopardy.

Recently, Shakeel was featured in *Ismaili Canada* for all his accomplishments: first place in Toronto's Annual Sci-Tech Fair, best attendance for Mission Class, most funds raised for World Partnership Walk (in his age category), top class honours at the provincial championship for Junior Toastmasters and Most Valuable Player for his team, Africana Lions, in the Midgets Ismaili Ball Hockey League. (Arif had sponsored the team since its inception; on the team uniforms' sleeves—"Dr. Arif Somani Makes Your Whole Family Smile.") Arif had cut out the article and placed it on the fridge, next to the calendar, each day marked with the various ceremonies they had to attend at jamatkhana (besides Friday evening prayers) and Shakeel's weekly activities.

When Arif and his brother were growing up, their parents owned a medium-sized grocery store located not far from the Dundas West subway station. The boys would go to the store after school and on weekends, doing their homework by themselves in the back room as their parents helped customers, shelved products, mopped the floor. His parents were always so busy with the store. They attended parent-teacher interviews and rewarded him for bringing home good report card, but they never had time for any extracurricular activities—Arif's soccer games or school plays. Arif understood that his parents were strangers in a new country and that their priority had to be the business, so he learned early on that he had to rely on himself. But, once in a moment of anger, Arif confronted them about their lack of involvement in his life, telling them they were unworthy parents and that they had no idea how much their children were suffering. His father never reprimanded him for his outburst. Instead, he had just said, "What can I do? We're doing all this for your benefit, *bheta*." Arif did not want the same childhood for his son. He wanted Shakeel to know his father and he wanted to be a father who was fully present—a term he had learned from reading *Today's Parent* and from listening to Dr. Phil's advice on *Oprah*. (There were TVs installed above each dental chair, for Arif's patients' comfort.)

"Please, *dhikro*," Sultan Uncle urged. "Listen to me. You won't enjoy camping one little bit."

"There's no way I'm going to go camping. I just won't do it." Meena swung one leg over the other, dangling her cork-heeled sandal off her raised foot.

"Wow. There's no winning against a united army." Arif was disappointed in Meena. There had been a time when she had been so much more open to new ideas. She wasn't an athlete like him, but even still, she willingly went on ski trips with him or took up running as a way for them to spend time together. It was her "get up and go" attitude that had attracted him to her in the first place. But over the years, Meena had become lazy. Arif accepted that she refused to work. But then the least he should expect was a well-managed household. There shouldn't be any excuse for not cooking every day or for keeping the house in tip-top shape—all four washrooms were rarely cleaned on a weekly basis. Arif never asked, but he often wondered what Meena did with all her time.

"Excellent. You won't regret it. You will enjoy yourselves immensely. This I know for sure." Sultan Uncle rolled his chair toward the windowed wall, which separated his office from the reception area, and wrapped his knuckles on the one-way glass. "This way, I can keep an eye on the operation. Otherwise they'd have their fingers up their asses, doing nothing all day."

No one responded to the knock. "See what I mean? These people, they're useless, absolutely useless."

Sultan Uncle pushed back his chair and stood up. He walked with a slight limp, one palm on the small of his back, his heavy belly hanging over his pants. A large wooden *tasbih* dangled from the fingers of his right hand. He leaned into the reception area and said something harshly in Swahili before returning to his chair.

Soon after, Fumo, Sultan Uncle's driver, came into the office. He removed his Chicago Bulls baseball cap and nodded at Meena and Arif. He wore a pair of jeans and a loose white T-shirt with a large decal of Princess Diana.

Fumo explained why he was late to Sultan Uncle. He had had trouble with the combie on the safari that he had just returned from. He apologized several times, his eyes darting from one wall to another.

"Oh yes, of course, the combie is useless." Sultan Uncle said, running his palm over his pitch-dark hair and wiping the oil off on a handkerchief. "All the time, one excuse or the other, hanh? This time, the combie. Next time what? Your dead mother?" He shook his head. "There are lineups for your job, lineups I am telling you, and still you don't want to listen. How many bloody chances can I give you?"

Fumo looked down and bent the visor of his baseball cap between his two hands.

Sultan Uncle pointed his pen at Fumo and addressed Arif. "Would you tolerate this in Canada? Never. Of course not. But this is what I have to deal with day in day out. How much can one man tolerate? Believe you me, if it wasn't for them, this country would be far more advanced. More advanced than even America. But problem is they want everything easy-*kama*-easy. Lazy bastards! Learn by example I say. How is it our people came to this country with hardly anything and built such empires? Simple. Hard work. Hard bloody work. But these people, they are born lazy and they will die lazy."

A black fly buzzed near Arif's ear. He swatted it away. He felt an over-whelming sense of pity for Fumo. He wished Fumo would say something, stand up for himself, refuse to be treated with such disdain. That was the only way to make change. Take things into your own hands. After all these years, Arif thought, not much had changed in Africa. A picture of Giselle, his childhood nanny, formed in his mind. Arif was playing in his bedroom when he heard a loud wail followed by a door slamming. Arif's mother had locked Giselle in the hallway closet and refused to let her out until she confessed to stealing a cup of *dhar* and some eggs from the pantry. Arif slipped some Digestive cookies under the door, but Giselle flatly refused. "You go, tell your mother I must use the toilet. Otherwise I leave a mountain of shit in here."

Arif rushed outside to the verandah where his mother was sitting on a small stool, separating stones from rice. His mother shook her head. "Let her try. Then we'll see what I'll do to her."

Arif's mother released Giselle an hour later. She rushed out and into the bathroom. Arif's mother banged on the door, threatening Giselle. She was not allowed to use their bathroom. She was supposed to go outside to the servants' quarters. Giselle stayed in the bathroom until Arif's father came home and coaxed her out, promising that nothing would happen to her. After Giselle finished her day's chores, she was fired. The next morning, Arif's mother hired a new ayah and supervised the *fundi* as he installed new locks on all the cupboards.

Arif knew he couldn't say anything to Sultan Uncle, especially in front of Shakeel. Children learned by example and he did not want to teach Shakeel that it was all right to talk back to elders. But the least he could do was protect his son from this nonsense. "Please Sultan Uncle," Arif interjected, titling his head toward Shakeel.

"Ah *shabaash, bheta*. What is wrong if the boy listens? Let him learn once and for all what Africa is all about. Thank God you got out when you did." Sultan Uncle took a bite out of a samosa. Some ground meat spilled out of the side of his mouth; he tried to stop it with a finger and stuff it back in. "But your father, he's too easily influenced. I told him back then, don't listen to all the fear mongering at jamatkhana. What the hell can Idi Amin do to us? We're in Kenya not Uganda. But did he listen? No. Instead he followed the entire bloody lot of them—scrambling to new countries like a bunch of pigeons to crumbs. And what all for? So you can be treated like second-class citizens. What kind of man would stand for that? I'm telling you, *bana*, it would have been far better if he had stayed put. Besides, what kind of crazy person prefers living in a deep freeze instead of this top-class climate, hanh?" Sultan Uncle turned back to Fumo. "And come tomorrow at six AM sharp. My family here want to go on safari. Masai Mara."

"Hotel or camping style?"

Sultan Uncle shook his head. "See what I mean? Nothing in here," he drummed two fingers to his forehead. "Hotel of course. Now go. And don't think for one second that the cost of the repairs is not coming straight out from your pay."

Fumo squeezed his cap flat between two hands. "*Sawa*, okay."

"If I hear one more excuse from you"—Sultan Uncle leaned back in his chair and wagged his finger at Fumo—"by God, it will be the end of you."

The creases of Fumo's eyelids quivered as if he had something caught in his eye. He nodded, then turned and left the office.

◆ ◆ ◆

"Mummy!" Shakeel yelled as he struggled to climb into the combie while holding a bunch of ripe bananas and his disposable camera. His floppy sun hat had fallen down over his glasses and one of the straps of his Ninja Turtles backpack had slipped off his shoulder.

"Oh, for God's sake," Meena said. She put her bottle of Fanta between her thighs; the straw, which was stained with a circle of fuchsia lipstick, bobbed up and down in the orange liquid. "Give me those." She reached for the bananas and then turned to Arif. "Why'd you buy so many? As if we'll even see any monkeys."

"Of course we will. We always did when we were kids." Arif lifted Shakeel into the combie. "There you go, buddy." Arif had never been on a proper safari to see the more majestic animals like the lion or leopard, but on their way from Nairobi to Bamburi Beach for their annual family vacation, he had seen countless animals on the road—giraffes, gazelles, zebras, monkeys. They would stop several times on the five-hour trip to the coast, to go swimming or to eat lunch at a hotel, but the highlight for Arif was stopping to feed the monkeys. Arif's father would park the car at the side of the road and before long troops of monkeys or baboons would gather, hooting and bouncing off the car. Arif and his brother would inch open the window and throw out the bananas, one at a time.

Meena pulled her sunglasses off her head. "That was a long time ago. Things must have changed. With all the filth and pollution here, the people are barely living. What about the poor monkeys?"

Arif asked Fumo about the likelihood of seeing monkeys before reaching the Masai Mara Game Park. "Maybe, bwana. It is all depending on our luck." Fumo slipped a cassette into the stereo socket. Bob Marley's *Get Up, Stand Up* blared from the speaker.

"I have a feeling that our chances are good." Arif turned to his son. "So it's your job to spot them, buddy. If you see any, let the driver know. Okay?"

Shakeel nodded enthusiastically. He turned on his knees and planted his palms on the window. His bright yellow camera, which was now strapped around his neck, clinked on the glass.

"Careful," Meena warned, pulling Shakeel back down.

"But it's disposable, Mummy. It can't break." Arif had purchased the camera in a bulk package of ten from Wal-Mart. This way, he told Shakeel, he could document his trip. Won't it be so much fun to show your friends? Shakeel agreed. Arif then spoke to Shakeel's teacher, Mrs. Henry. She agreed. It would an excellent learning opportunity for the students. When they returned from Kenya, Shakeel would make a slide presentation to the class entitled "Shakeel Somani: Where I Come From."

The combie raced along the rocky and unpaved road to Masai Mara. Fumo expertly manoeuvred around the potholes; even so, they were often bumped out of their seats.

"Incredible, hmm?" Arif said, leaning into Meena and pointing to the rolling foothills of the Great Rift Valley.

Shakeel's camera whirred as he snapped picture after picture.

"Hmm," Meena said, fanning herself with a copy of her *Vogue*, one of the magazines she had taken from the plane. "Could you please turn on the aircon?" Meena asked Fumo.

Fumo fumbled with some knobs. A blast of hot air shot out and then stopped. "Aye. I am very sorry, mamma. It is not working."

"God, does anything work in this country?" Meena said and flipped open *Cosmopolitan.*

Arif rolled down the window. "This should help." He leaned forward toward Fumo, his elbows on his knees. "You have been working for Twiga Travel a long time?" he asked, meeting Fumo's eyes in the rearview mirror.

"Yes, sir. Maybe seven years. I come from a small village close to Narok. You know it?"

Arif shook his head.

"We will pass it by. It is on the way to the park. But I am coming to Nairobi for work, you see."

"Do you have kids?"

"Yes, yes. I am a blessed man. Five. Three boys and two girls," Fumo said, smiling. "They are staying in Narok. I am coming and going. When it is high touristic time, I am coming to Nairobi."

Five kids! How could Fumo support such a big family and all by himself? Fumo seemed so young, twenty-five at the most. "You should start your own travel agency, Fumo," Arif said, remembering the terrible assault Fumo endured in Sultan Uncle's office. "Work for yourself. That is the only way to get ahead, you know. And you shouldn't let anything come in your way. Just take charge."

Fumo laughed. "Yes, okay, sir. Maybe, one day I will save enough money and then I will open my own business. Ah, but your uncle, he is a good man. He give me job all this time."

"Don't rely on anyone, Fumo. No one. You can only count on yourself."

Fumo shrugged his shoulders. "Yes, okay."

Arif felt good that perhaps he had planted a seed in Fumo's mind. How else would he survive, support such a big family. "So is this the best time to go on safari?"

"Oh yes, bwana. Any time is a good time, hanh." Fumo described how, in a few months, there would be a mass migration of wildebeest from the Serengeti. "They stay here for some months. Eating, eating. Then they are going back. All the time, here and there. Here and there. They have no home, you see. Always on safari." Fumo smiled into the rearview mirror. "They are like me, hanh?"

There was yet another reason Fumo needed to get into business. "I could help you, you know." Arif offered. "I could help you with a business plan. I'm a dentist."

"A dentist, hanh?" Fumo paused for a moment and then tilted the rearview mirror toward himself. "Maybe, bwana, you can remove this." Fumo pointed deep inside his mouth to a molar. "It is causing me too much pain."

"Ah, but I don't have any of equipment here."

"I have pliers, sir. Is that helping?"

"No, no. I couldn't use that. Besides, it's not like I have a dental licence here. But listen, I can definitely help you draft a business plan."

"Okay," Fumo said, his eyebrows knitted together. He titled the rearview mirror back in place.

"You think we'll see the big five on safari?"

"Ah yes. You will see the all the big animals. No problem, bwana. But next time, you must come for the wildebeest. So many animals in one place and only one purpose. "

"Is that when most of the tourists come?"

"The tourists, they are coming all the time. From all over the world, they come here to Kenya. We are very lucky." Fumo looked up and into the rearview mirror at Arif. "And you, sir, you are from where?"

"Well, I was born here," Arif said proudly. "But we live in Toronto. We'd like to come back here to retire." Arif liked the idea of spending his last days here, of being buried in the country of his birth.

Meena mumbled something as she turned a page of her magazine.

"Oh I see. Canada. Yes, I have people from there also. It is very cold there, yes? In wintertime, you watch ice hockey. You like this very much. But you do not like the French people. They are causing you too much trouble."

Arif smiled. "You know a lot about Canada, hey?"

"I am learning from my customers."

"See, you already have a customer base. You're well on your way to starting a business."

"Maybe you are right, sir. I have many friends everywhere." Fumo tapped his head. "You see this hat? My friend, George, he is living in Chicago. He send me this. Chicago Bulls. He like basketball very much."

"Now you have a friend in Toronto."

"Yes, yes." Fumo smiled and met Arif's eyes in the rearview mirror.

"Me, I love Shaq. Best player in the league. Who do you think my son is named after?" Arif laughed. "You like basketball, Fumo?"

"I do not know how to play. But I like America. One day, maybe I will go there. They make everything very nice."

"Well, I could send you a Toronto Maple Leafs T-shirt or even a jersey." Arif paused. "Not that they ever win," he laughed. "Not since 1967."

Fumo shook his head. "I am sorry for such bad news, sir. It is terrible."

Arif nodded. When Arif was growing up he had rooted for the Maple Leafs, but after years of cheering and nothing to show for it, he decided to cheer to switch allegiances to the Edmonton Oilers. He watched as they slowly rose up to be the best team in the league. Hard work and perseverance—it was the only surefire way to success! A combination the Leafs never seemed to get straight.

But when Wayne Gretzky was traded to Los Angeles, Arif had felt so betrayed that he tore all his Gretzky cards into little pieces and threw them down the toilet. As he flushed, he vowed never to watch Gretzsky play again. Arif and Shakeel were avid hockey fans, but to this day, even though Gretzky was retired, Arif insisted Shakeel turn the TV off when the Los Angeles Kings were playing.

• • •

The combie sped ahead, passing a boy on a bicycle, a goat strapped to the handlebars, and many women—some with their babies tied around them with kanga cloth, tilling the fields, others walking on the side of the road with baskets on their heads, and lines of barefoot children in tattered clothes. The children screamed and waved as the combie drove by.

"See how lucky we are to live in Canada?" Arif said to Shakeel.

"Did you used have to bicycle with a goat too?"

Arif laughed. "No. But these kids hardly have anything to eat. It's just very hard for them." Arif tapped Fumo's shoulder. "Is it all right if we stop? We'd like to meet the children."

Fumo turned the stereo volume down. *One Love* was now barely audible. "But, sir, they will only ask you for money."

"That's fine." Arif wanted Shakeel to have as many first-hand experiences as possible.

Meena looked up from her magazine. "What for, Arif? At this rate we'll never get to the hotel."

"It'll only take a few minutes."

Fumo veered onto the shoulder and stopped the vehicle. The children rushed to the vehicle. Their noses were blocked with thick mucous and their stomachs bloated.

"Hello, sir, hello," they chanted, each of them scrambling to get their hands into the open window.

Meena pulled away. "Shoo, shoo," she shrieked, waving them away.

"One shilling please. One shilling."

Fumo stepped outside and tried to control the clamour. He swatted the children's heads and pulled one of the boys off the vehicle. The boy had gripped the inside of the combie through an open window and was trying to climb in.

"No, Fumo," Arif said. "Please, don't hit them. They're only children."

Fumo stood aside.

Arif tried to engage the children in a conversation. He introduced Shakeel to them, asked them where they lived, what they liked to do for fun. But the children were single-minded. They wanted a shilling.

"Good God, just give them some money and get it over with," Meena said, twisting her watch around her wrist.

"Money's the easy solution," Arif retorted. Who knows what they would do with the money? Buy beer or drugs?" Arif preferred to give them food. He reached for the bananas, snapped one off, and offered it to the children.

"But the monkeys, Daddy!"

"It's okay, buddy. We'll get more."

The children refused the bananas.

"See how ungrateful they are," Meena said. "Just give them the money. What's a few shilling to us? A few cents, if that"

One of the children pointed to a stall. "Milk."

Fumo warned that the children would only sell the milk for money. "No," Arif said. "They need milk for healthy teeth and bones." He escorted Shakeel and the rest of the children, each of them fighting to hold Arif's hand, to the confectionary stall. He purchased a triangular packet of powdered milk for each of them.

"Thank you, sir," the children screamed.

"You are very welcome." Arif said, feeling a deep sense of accomplishment.

One of the girls tugged at the camera hanging around Shakeel's neck. "No!" Shakeel pulled back so forcefully that he yanked the girl forward. "It's mine."

Meena beeped the horn. Arif looked over to see her figure in an l shape as she reached forward from the back seat and over the driver's seat.

"Hurry, take a picture, buddy." Arif gestured to the children, pointing to Shakeel's camera. They seemed to understand what he meant. They giggled, struggling with each other as they each tried for the front row.

Shakeel held the camera awkwardly with both hands and snapped a picture; the faces of children wide open with laughter.

◆ ◆ ◆

Soon after they had eaten lunch at a small restaurant, the combie began to gurgle. It rolled forward a few inches, rocked back, and then stopped.

Fumo cranked the gears and tried to restart the combie, but nothing. It was dead.

"What's wrong?" Arif asked.

"It is okay. I fix it. No problem."

Fumo lifted the cover of what seemed like a large armrest between the front two seats. He tinkered with some wires and levers, then slapped the dashboard. "We must let the engine cool it down, that is all."

As they waited, a group of Masai women wearing colourful, printed wraps and adorned with thick, beaded jewellery—necklaces, earrings, lip and nose rings—rushed toward them from the other side of the road. Their arms were filled with wooden carvings.

Arif pointed to the women. "There's a picture for you, buddy." Shakeel clambered onto the seat and readied his camera.

Fumo tapped the rearview mirror. "Please, bwana, no picture. The Masai, they do not like it. They are feeling that the photo steal their soul."

"Come on, really?" Arif asked.

"Yes, it is true. And if she see you, she will ask for money. Not shillings, bwana. No, no. Only American dollars." He laughed. "You see, free trade has reached us here in Kenya even."

The women shouted excitedly, thrusting their wares into the open window of the combie. "Jambo! So nice. Good price."

"Take a look, Meena. They look beautiful"

Meena shook her head and waved her hand at the women. "Forget it. Let's wait until we get to the hotel. I'm sure they'll have a gift shop."

But Arif was suddenly intrigued with a thin black carving of a Masai family, the woman cradling an infant and the man standing behind them with spear. "How much?" he asked, leaning over Meena and pointing to the statue.

The woman turtled behind the combie and appeared at his window. Meena rolled up her window. The other women left to sit at the side of the road.

"For you, bwana, special price. How much you like?"

"Oh, I don't know. Maybe three hundred shillings?"

"How many you take?"

"Just that one."

"No, no. Too small price. Five hundred shilling."

"Five hundred shillings?" Meena asked. "That's outrageous. I'm sure I saw some in Nairobi for much less. Don't waste your time with her."

Arif turned back to the woman, shrugged his shoulders. "Three hundred shillings."

Fumo tried to start the vehicle again. The engine roared back to life.

The woman shoved the carving into Arif's hand. "*Basi, bana*. Three hundred shilling."

Arif ran his finger up and down the crevices of the statue. It was smooth and delicate, yet it felt strong. The craftsmanship was impeccable. "I'm sure it's ebony," he said and handed it to Meena. "Take a look. It's terrific."

Meena examined the statue. She pushed her thumb into the faces, then turned it upside down and wrapped her knuckles to the base a few times. "No, it feels fragile. It might break before we get it home. Don't let her take advantage. Offer two hundred shillings max."

The woman pulled back the kanga slung around her to show her baby, his nose dripping, his eyes yellowed. She cupped the baby's chin. "Me mamma. You mamma. Please. Three hundred shilling."

Meena looked away, tucked a strand of loose hair behind her ear. "Two hundred shillings. That's our final offer."

As Fumo stepped on the gas, the woman reached in and grabbed Arif's wrist. "Please, bwana. Three hundred shilling."

Fumo beeped the horn. He then turned back and said something to the women in Swahili and tried to wave her away. The woman refused to leave.

Meena snatched the statue from Arif's grip and threw it out the window. "No means no!" Meena tapped the back of Fumo's seat. "Let's go. We're done here."

Fumo started to drive away. The woman leaned down and picked up the statue. She chased the combie, running next to it, the carving held high above her, her baby bouncing up and down. "*Basi, bana*, two hundred shilling. Between hundred shilling!" But the combie was rattling ahead at full speed. Arif turned back to see the woman shrinking so that soon she was only a speck in the far distance. Suddenly, he felt angry. What was Meena teaching Shakeel? That it was all right to treat people unfairly? He would have to make it a point to discuss the matter with her when they arrived at the hotel. He did not want to start an argument in front of Shakeel.

"Sir, if you like I can take you to my village," Fumo suggested, his head cocked back as he looked at Arif in the rearview mirror. "My friend, Patrick, he have a nice shop. You will find very good carvings there. It is all locally made. Better price than this lady."

"The village it is close by," Fumo continued. "Just before Masai Mara. If you like, we will also make a tour of my village afterward."

"Really? What a great idea." Arif turned to Meena and Shakeel. "So what do you guys think? It would our chance to see a real African village."

"Yeah, Dad. I'll get lots of good pictures."

"Forget it," Meena said. "The sooner we get to the hotel, the better."

"Come on, Meena. Who gets to shop in the jungle?" Arif joked, slipping his fingers under her T-shirt and tickling her stomach. "It will be an adventure. And I'm sure we'll get excellent prices. Isn't that right Fumo? You'll be able to get us a good discount, won't you?"

"Yes, of course, bwana. No problem. You are my friend now. I will make sure you get big discount." Fumo said, tapping the steering wheel to the rhythm of *Buffalo Soldier.*

Arif raised his eyebrows to Meena. "See?"

"Okay, fine," Meena said, smiling. She moved Arif's hand to her thigh and pulled down her T-shirt.

"That's my girl." Arif leaned in and kissed Meena. "Full speed ahead, Captain Fumo. Narok it is."

• • •

Shakeel turned back on his knees, planted his chin on the backrest and stared outside.

"Daddy, when are we going to see the monkeys? We haven't seen any yet."

"Soon, buddy. I'm sure of it." Just as Arif reached up and rustled Shakeel's hair, he saw something, monkeys perhaps, moving in the bushes. "Stop, Fumo!"

Fumo braked suddenly, throwing Shakeel forward and down onto the floor of the vehicle. Meena was jolted forward. Arif braced himself. The combie screeched to a halt.

Shakeel sat on the floor, his arms and legs tangled. Arif quickly reached down and lifted his son onto his lap. "You okay, buddy?"

"Give him to me," Meena reached over and grabbed Shakeel. "Oh God. You okay, sweetheart?" She held him by the shoulders and examined his face.

"What's wrong with you, driver?" Meena yelled. "You almost had us all killed."

Fumo turned around, apologizing profusely, his hands together in prayer.

Arif felt a surge of frustration and anger rise in him. Why can't this man just stand up for himself? He has no idea, but he would be such a different person if he only learned to be confident instead of constantly cowering to others. "Stop apologizing, Fumo! I'm the one who made you stop. I'm sure I saw some monkeys."

"Where, where?" Shakeel said, as he scrambled for camera.

Arif rolled down his window and pointed to the dense bush. "Let's see if we can get their attention." Arif hooted, his back hunched over, fingers under his armpits.

"You're funny, Daddy." Shakeel giggled.

Fumo turned back to Arif. "Sir, we must go."

"No. Let's wait a little while. We just got here."

Fumo pointed to three men approaching from the distance.

"Who are they?"

Fumo shook his head. He cranked the gears and stepped on the accelerator. The combie zoomed by the men. All three were in jeans and fatigued army jackets, scarves tied around their necks. They carried rifles strapped across their backs. One of the men walked with a pronounced limp.

Shakeel poked his head out the window and snapped a picture.

"No!" Meena yanked him back down. "You'll hurt yourself again."

"But Mom, they look like Ninja Turtles."

"Sit down. And put that stupid camera away for God's sake."

Fumo changed gears. The combie began to sputter, gurgling for a few seconds as it began to slow.

Meena swung her head back to the men. "Don't stop!"

The combie came to a full stop.

Arif turned to see the men approaching. "Who are they?" His mouth suddenly dried. His hands shook slightly as he reached for a bottle of water.

"Go!" Meena ordered. "Those hoodlums are getting closer."

"Ninjas, Mom, not hoodlums."

Fumo tried to turn the engine, but it would not budge. One of the men slapped his palm to the driver side door. "What is the hurry, my friend?" he asked, smiling, his top two front teeth glinted gold. He opened the driver's side door, leaned in and peered over Fumo's head and into the back of the combie. He said something to Fumo in Swahili. Fumo shook his head. He reached in past the stereo and turned it off. He ejected the cassette of Bob Marley and slipped it into his shirt pocket.

Arif silently wished for Fumo to fight back, to do something. Don't just stand there. The only way to get respect was to command it.

The first man, whom Arif mentally named Goldteeth, walked to the side door and flung it open. Meena leaned back. He stepped one foot in and leaned an elbow on his knee. A toothpick dangled from the side of his mouth. "Jambo. Karibuni Kenya. Welcome to this great land." He smiled.

One of the men jumped onto the hood and sprawled out, one leg hanging over the side of the vehicule.

Fumo stepped out of the combie. The third man grabbed him by the shoulder and easily pushed him aside. The men laughed. "Could you tell us why you've stopped us?" Arif asked with what he hoped sounded like confidence. "We don't want any trouble."

Goldteeth turned to his cohorts. "You hear this? The man is saying we want to make trouble? Is that true or false?"

"False," the men chanted. One of the men, a pink Band-Aid taped across his cheekbone, lit a cigarette, took a long slow drag, and then titled his head back and blew out the smoke.

"This is a border crossing here," Goldteeth continued, moving the tooth-pick between two teeth. "You have to pay the toll. It is a regulation of the Kenyan government. Nothing we can do."

"A border crossing?"

"Yes, you are now on our land. All foreigners, they must pay. It is a touristic tax, you see. A head tax." He ran his tongue over his front teeth.

"But we're not foreigners. I was born here." Arif said matter-of-factly.

"Just give him some money," Meena whispered angrily.

"Is that right?" Goldteeth leaned back outside to his partners. "We do not have foreigners here. We have our brethren." He turned his gaze back into the combie. "So, my friend, this is your home, hanh?"

"Yes," Arif said, encouraged "This was one of the main reasons we came here. I wanted my son to learn more about his history. To understand his roots."

"I see," Goldteeth pursed his lips and nodded. "But you are living in America, no?"

"Canada."

"You can come and go anytime, hanh? That is very nice for you." Goldteeth pointed to Shakeel with his toothpick. "What is your name, *bana kidogo*, little boss?"

"Shakeel," Shakeel said, adjusting his glasses.

Goldteeth reached in to examine the camera around Shakeel's neck. Shakeel was forced forward.

"No!" Shakeel screamed, pulling back. "That's my project for school!"

Goldteeth dropped the camera, raised his palms. "Okay, okay! Your son, he is like a lion."

Yes, he had a strong son, Arif thought. "Go ahead, buddy. Tell the man your project."

Arif hoped that hearing the story might help pacify the man.

Shakeel explained the project and the purpose of the camera. "And Mrs. Henry, um, she said that she liked my idea best of all. She even gave me an extra gold star. 'Cause not all the kids can teach other kids something special. I can teach them all about Africa."

"Oye-yo-yo, *bana kidogo*." Goldteeth shook his head. "You are smart. An expert on Africa, hmm?"

The man on the hood of the car banged a fist to the windshield and said something in Swahili. Goldteeth shook his head and waved his hand.

"Is everything all right?" Arif asked.

"Yes, everything, it is fine. He is only impatient. He want to go home. His woman, she is waiting." Goldteeth winked and then tilted his head toward Meena. "Big trouble if you keep her waiting too long, hanh?" he laughed.

Arif laughed, but stopped when he saw the scowl on Meena's face.

Fumo stood up and tried to say something. The man with a limp punched him in the stomach. He planted both palms to Fumo's shoulder and pushed him into the ditch.

Goldteeth waved Shakeel forward. "Come, *bana kidogo.*"

"No!" Arif said, holding Shakeel back.

"Aye, bwana. I will not harm him."

Arif maintained his grip on his son. "But what do you want?"

Goldteeth shook his head and laughed. "There is a new school in my village. But we have no teacher, you see. Maybe your son, he can teach the children." Goldteeth beckoned Shakeel forward. "Come, do not be so scared."

Just as Shakeel looked to Arif for permission, Goldteeth ducked into the combie and snatched Shakeel out of Arif's arms.

"No!" Meena screamed.

Arif rushed behind, his arms outstretched. "Please. We don't want any problems."

"Ah, but this is Africa, it is filled with problems, yes? Let us try to solve one today." Goldteeth turned and made a line in the gravel with his heel. He placed Shakeel behind the line. "If I am to hire your son, I must first see how smart he is. " He motioned to the other men. "Eh, Rafiki. Come. Maybe you are learning something. This boy, he is expert. He know everything about Africa."

"But he's too little. He can't be a teacher!" Meena cried, clutching her purse.

"This isn't fair," Arif said.

The other men including Fumo were made to sit on the other side of the line, across Shakeel.

Goldteeth waved his gun in the air. "Attention class, attention. Your new school is about to open. So many children, they have no school. But today, you are lucky. You must pay attention. We have here," he pointed to Shakeel with his gun, "an expert. He will teach us. Come, let us begin." Goldteeth leaned into his rifle like a cane.

"*Bana kidogo*, can you tell the class what year Kenya is finally getting our independence? Uhuru at last!"

Shakeel raised his eyebrows, shrugged his shoulders.

Goldteeth bent down and cupped Shakeel's head in his hand. "You must try, little boss." Shakeel twisted his lips to one side. He looked to his parents.

"Please! " Meena screamed.

"I am waiting, little boss." Goldteeth paced the line between Shakeel and his students.

"I dunno."

"Oh, *bana kidogo*! Did I not say, you must try? That is the most important thing. You disappoint me too much." Goldteeth leaned down and slapped Shakeel across the mouth.

Shakeel cupped his mouth and started wailing.

"No!" Arif stepped forward, his heart filled with a mix of anger and fear. "Please, I beg you. Don't do this."

"Do something, Arif. Do something!" Meena cried.

Shakeel was now crying uncontrollably.

"Please. I will do anything. Give you anything you want."

"What can you give me?" Goldteeth asked.

Arif removed all the bills in his wallet and offered them to Goldteeth. "Please, take this." Goldteeth did not budge. Arif rushed back to the combie and seized Meena's purse. He held the bright pink handbag to Goldteeth. To Arif's relief, Goldteeth took it. He held the purse, the strap bunched in his fist like the neck of a dead chicken. He then dropped it. It hit the ground with a thud. "It is always the same thing with you people, hanh? Money. Money. Money. You think you can have anything if you have money."

"I will give you anything. Please just leave my son."

Goldteeth poked the butt of his rifle into Arif's shoulder and pushed him back. "The class is not over." He turned back to Shakeel. "Let us try again. Concentrate. I give you an easy one this time. Can you name for me, *bana kidogo,* one member of the Mau Mau movement or even GEMA of today?"

"Daddy!" Shakeel sniffled, wiping his tears away with dusty hands. "Help me!"

Goldteeth turned to Arif, raised his eyebrows. "Okay, okay. Come. Come help him. He is your son after all. And I am not a monster."

Arif rushed forward. He bent down and slipped his hands under Shakeel's arms. Goldteeth pushed him away. He wagged his finger at him. "No, you cannot take him. Answer for him. If you know the answer then he will be spared his punishment."

"Please!" Arif dropped to his knees. "Please, do not do this to us."

"Ah, but, sir. This is your country. You cannot answer such a simple question about our history? Your people, they have been here a long time, no? Please, you must only answer the question. All you must do is name one member of the independence movement. Only one. It is a simple matter really."

Arif put his hands together in prayer. "Please. This is impossible."
Goldteeth struck Shakeel across the head. He screamed.

Fumo suddenly rushed forward in two giant steps and pounced on Goldteeth.

Meena ran out of the combie. She grabbed Shakeel and hurried him back to the vehicle. "Are you okay, sweetheart?" She asked frantically, patting down his hair.

Fumo and Goldteeth rolled over each other on the ground, each grabbing and punching at the other.

"Stop!" the man with the limp yelled, pointing his rifle at Fumo.

Arif pushed himself up from the ground and ran to the combie, slamming the door shut behind him. He locked all the doors and then climbed, one leg after the other, into the driver's seat. The man with the Band-Aid charged toward the combie.

"Hurry!" Meena cried, her hands wrapped around Shakeel's head as she pulled him into her chest. Shakeel was still crying, his mouth bleeding on Meena's T-shirt, mumbling, "My camera, Mummy. My camera."

The man hammered the end of his rifle to the driver side window.

Arif's fingers fumbled with the key in the ignition. He turned the engine over and over again, desperately trying to make it work.

A gunshot fired.

"Go!" Meena screamed, shielding Shakeel's eyes. "Go!"

The combie suddenly sputtered back to life. Arif shoved the gearshift into drive and then pressed down on the the gas pedal. The glare of the hot African sun glinted in the rearview mirror. He turned the mirror up and away, keeping his gaze focused on the road straight ahead as he sped away.

Birthday Blues
Pratap Reddy

1.

I woke up on the morning of my twelfth birthday and immediately wished I hadn't. It was almost ten and the house had that deathly Sunday stillness. I went to the washroom, peed, wiped the seat clean of the yellow drops and flushed the toilet—all as mum had trained me to do.

I went back to my room and picked up *The Dark Knight Returns*. I lay down on my bed and began to read. Reading kept my mind off things like how dorky all my birthdays have been. Okay, not all, but at least the ones I can remember. I needed no crystal ball to tell me that today would be no different.

I heard a sudden *vroom* downstairs—mum must have started on her favourite weekend pastime, vacuuming the whole damn universe. It was only a matter of time before she came upstairs, dragging the machine like a pit bull on a leash. I got up and played Back Street Boys real loud to drown the racket she was making.

Soon enough, without so much as a knock, mum pushed open my bedroom door. Mum believed in surprising people.

"There's no *need* to put on the music that loud," she said.

I got up and tweaked the controls—pretending to reduce the volume. It had been an entirely different ball game when Joe was around.

Mum shut the door and I went back to my book. A couple of seconds later, she opened the door again.

"Happy birthday, son. What would you like to do today?"

What would I like to do? Go bowling with my buddies, Tony and Mustapha, that's what. But I kept that thought to myself. Extreme caution—if you know what I mean.

"Shall we go to the temple?" mum asked brightly. I wanted to groan. She continued: "First, I'll make some food for your dad."

Dad had died two years ago, exactly on the same date. Last year, mum cooked for him and placed the food below his framed photograph on the wall. Later, we ate the leftovers—some birthday treat.

Don't get me wrong: dad had been a good dude. I wouldn't say the same thing of Joe. Though dad could be cantankerous at times, he was a chummy kind of person. If I did something stupid, he'd roll his eyes and say, *Je-sus*! He used to say that all the time even though he was a full-blown Hindu, born and bred in India.

Mum too was born in India. But you wouldn't have guessed, looking at her. She always wore stuff like tops and pants, and her hair was cut very short. Even her accent didn't sound Indian (nor did it sound very Canadian).

Dad's parents had seen mum in a photograph that a relative had sent them from India. In the picture, mum was wearing a sari, and she had flowers in her long hair and a big red dot on her forehead. According to mum, my grandparents took such a shine to her that they boarded the next plane to India and arranged dad's marriage. When mum came to Canada, nobody would give her a job. She had to go to college again and take ESL classes before she finally managed to find work in a dental office.

After mum finally left the room, I got back to my book. I liked reading—I devoured graphic novels by the ton. When I grow up I'd like to be a writer. I like words. Nice long words, words that have a majestic ring to them. Unfortunately, my spelling sucked. Miss Bowman, my class teacher said that you must know how to spell if you wanted to be a writer.

"No sweat," Tony said. "You can always use the spell check."

But Mustapha said, "Only ninnies use spell check, duh."

2.

On the evening of my tenth birthday, dad tried to knot a bowtie around my neck. Unlike mum, dad was tall and heavily built, with large clumsy hands. He appeared a little out of breath and droplets of sweat formed on his brow as he struggled with the tie. It was August and the weather was hot and stuffy. Mum never switched the AC on until the temperature touched one hundred degrees—Celsius, mind you, not Fahrenheit.

Mum had bought me a black pinstripe suit to wear to my birthday party at Chuck E. Cheese. When dad said that nobody wore a suit to Chuck E. Cheese, mum simply steamrollered over his objections—like always.

Mum had invited all her friends, her relatives and their children to the party. But Tony and Mustapha were nowhere in the guest list—you'd think it was mum's birthday party.

"Can't you tie a bowtie properly?" mum said to dad.

She roughly spun me in her direction and started to maniplate the bowtie. I was half-afraid I'd get strangled to death.

"It's loose. You'll have to tighten it," dad said.

That darn tie was choking me as it was.

"So you think you know everything, eh?" she asked of dad.

That's how it started. Before I could even get into my pinstripe coat, they were screaming at each other. Then came the usual Act Two, when things got physical—dad gave mum a slap on her shoulder. And mum replied in kind—with a sort of a punch in his stomach. I watched the bout mutely, like a referee who had misplaced his whistle.

They stopped fighting just as suddenly and got on with the job of getting ready as if nothing had happened—like they always did. But as dad was about to pick up his car keys, he gave out a loud moan—as though somebody was tying a bowtie very tightly around his throat. He fell down with a crash, breaking the leg of an end table. Mum screamed and dialled 911.

We accompanied dad in the ambulance because mum didn't know how to drive. I sat next to him in my pinstripe trousers and bowtie. Mum was continually on the mobile, calling her friends and relatives to cancel the party. The paramedic heard her and wished me a happy birthday. Dad looked at me, rolled his eyes and mouthed "*Je*-sus!"

When we got out of the ambulance we found that some of my parents' friends and relatives had decided to follow us to the hospital. Perhaps they wanted to give mum and dad moral support. Or did they think that the venue of the party had moved? Seeing the long lineup of cars—a preview of his funeral procession—must have unnerved dad.

He never got out of the hospital alive. I miss dad. I think he had loved me in his own peculiar way, whatever mum said to the contrary.

3.

It was a foregone conclusion that my eleventh birthday would be a no-go. After all it was dad's anniversary, too. Mum had been weepy for days. She said that she missed dad.

As a sparring partner, I thought. One way or another I couldn't see the two of us trying to restart the abandoned party at Chuck E. Cheese.

Mum made chicken tikka and fried rice and offered them to dad. They were his favourite Indian dishes. When we finally got to eat the food, it was stone cold.

"The food tastes funny," I said. "I think it needs some salt."

"That's right," mum said. "Dr. Moore had told me use less salt in the cooking because your dad was—what's the word?"

"Hypersensitive," I suggested.

"Whatever, but I never got around to doing it when your dad was alive," mum said.

In the evening we went to a temple. We took the bus because we didn't own a car. Mum hadn't yet met Joe. The temple was in a quiet neighbourhood but it had no dome or spire or anything. It could have been mistaken for an office block — I mean, it didn't even look Indian, like the Taj Mahal or something.

Inside, a wine-red carpet stretched from wall to wall. On a raised platform, life-size statues of Hindu deities sat in a row looking straight ahead, as though waiting to be introduced to the gathering. Mum walked up to each one of them with both her palms joined together, whispering all the while. I trailed behind her, doing a fair imitation of her actions and hoping that I too would look religious.

In a corner, a half-naked pujari sat on the floor distributing holy water and prasad. He spoke to us in Hindi. The priest looked newly arrived from India. A *jnaani*-come-lately, mum said. Mum thinks she's got a great sense of humour. That's the real joke, let me tell you.

On our way back, mum stopped at Wal-Mart. She bought a crappy boom-box as a birthday present for me. I wish she had bought me something cool like a PlayStation or a Game Boy. Something that would have made Tony's and Mustapha's jaws drop.

4.

Joginder was mum's instructor at *Singh Along Driving School for Ladies*. After helping her get a licence, Joe took the liberty of renting our basement. "To lighten our burden," mum said. "Besides, it's good for you to have a father figure around."

There's no denying we were hard up. Mum was doing mostly temp jobs. Even when she had a good job, she was constantly poring over the help wanted columns in newspapers. That's because she couldn't get along with her bosses—she found them too bossy.

Though Joe had rented only the basement, he was upstairs most of the time. Wearing a tacky golf shirt and a pair of shorts, he would strut about the house showing off his hairy limbs. He had a big bulge in his crotch as though he was carrying a pet turtle between his legs. A nice father figure he cut.

Very soon I realized that Joe was sneaking into mum's bedroom. I could hear him beyond the wall, whispering, giggling and indulging in other -ings. Whenever Joe was with mum, I turned on the boom-box full blast. Throwing music like a coverlet over my head, I'd try to go to sleep.

Not before long, even mum's patience with Joe began to wear thin. He never gave her any help around the house; repairing his car was all the work he did. Every weekend, he'd settle down in the driveway to repair his old Ford. That jalopy always gave trouble. Often we'd find ourselves sitting in the car, marooned in the middle of the road as Joe tried to fix something or the other under the hood.

But mum wasn't the kind to give up easily. She was constantly after Joe, wanting him to run errands for her. And Joe began to change—he'd disappear into his basement for long stretches, and whenever he emerged, he looked sullen and scrappy.

On Saturday morning, a day before my twelfth birthday, I woke up late. I heard Joe's steam-bellow snores in the bedroom next door. I got up and played Eminem on high. It flushed him out of the room in a blink.

"Buddy, why do you put on the music so loud?" Joe asked.

"I don't like the sounds you make in mum's room," I said.

If you thought my boom-box was loud, you hadn't heard the commotion that was going on in the kitchen. Mum had discovered that there were no groceries in the house even to prepare a light brunch. On Friday, before leaving for work, mum had given Joe a list of things to buy. But as usual he had forgotten all about it. Mum was raging mad that she had no choice but to take us out to lunch.

"Why don't we go to the fancy new Thai restaurant in Mississauga?" said Joe. I couldn't help admiring this guy.

"We're going to the *pho*," mum said, in a chilly no-nonsense voice.

If ever we needed to dine out, mum would always take us to a Vietnamese restaurant on Main Street and order the same dish for each one of us—a noodle soup with meatballs swimming in it. Mum had reckoned that for twenty dollars the three of us could eat our fill and still have some cash left-over for a generous tip.

Hearing about the *pho*, Joe burst out, "I'm sick and tired of eating item number eighteen every time!"

"Really?" mum started to say.

I recognized that tone. It was only a matter of time before mum would go ballistic. The next thing I knew, the two were in the middle of a slanging match. When it was time for Act Two, mum threw a punch at Joe. The poor man was taken aback. No woman other than his mother had ever smacked him.

Joe turned and, without a word, went down into his basement. He resurfaced twenty minutes later with a suitcase in one hand and a bunch of unwashed clothes in the crook of his other arm. "I'm outta here!" he said and walked out of the house, stopping only to bang the door after him.

The Ford coughed apologetically and refused to start at first. But eventually it did and, emitting a roar, the car sped away. Though I didn't like Joe, I felt kind of sad. For her part, mum picked up the *Star* and leafed through the entertainment section like it was any other lazy Saturday afternoon.

5.

So now, on my twelfth birthday, I saw no signs of any birthday present coming my way. I didn't care either—after all, I wasn't a kid anymore.

In the evening we went to the temple in an ancient Chevy Cavalier mum had bought, with expert advice from Joe, soon after she had learned how to drive. The highway was busy with the summer weekend rush. But I had to hand it to mum—she drove like a pro. Cohabiting with a driving instructor seemed to have had its own advantages.

The temple looked the same. But there was a poster on a wall now asking for donations to build a dome. In the main hall, the deities continued to sit and stare into the air. The priest was in his corner, fully dressed in a white kurta and pyjamas. He spoke to us in English, with a Canadian accent to boot. He must have hired a really good English tutor, I thought—somebody far better than Miss Bowman. But mum told me that he had married a white lady, a Hare Krishna devotee.

On our way back, mum put on the radio. The announcer came on the air, talking about floods in some remote part of the world. Mum pulled out a small bag from the glove box. Handing it me, she said, "Happy birthday!"

I was so flabbergasted, I forgot to thank her. While she was listening to the announcer yakking about a mine collapse, I opened the bag and peeked inside. My eyes must have surely popped out. An iPod Nano!

Mum shut off the radio and turned to me. "The things that happen on your birthday! Floods in Bangladesh, an accident in a Chinese mine and a hurricane blowing across the Caribbean!"

Turning a deaf ear to mum, I opened the package. Silver coloured and gleaming, how beautiful the iPod looked! I was extra careful as I pried out the device. When I held it in my hands, I was afraid I'd leave indelible fingerprints on it.

"I think your birthdays are truly jinxed," said mum.

"Me too," I said, absently.

I fished out the earphones and stuffed them into my ears. Though it would be some time before the iPod started pumping music into my ears, I was already beginning to feel happy with my life. I could hardly wait to tell Tony and Mustapha about my birthday present.

"Thank you, mum," I said. "You are the best!" I wanted to kiss her on her cheek, but held back because it would have been such an uncool thing to do.

Out of the blue, mum said: "Shall we go out for dinner?"

"Wh-where?" I asked, a vision of meatballs in a foggy soup rising in my mind.

"To the fancy new Thai restaurant in Mississauga," said mum, stepping on the gas.

Poems
Shauntay Grant

JAZZ FEST (FOR TRANE)

MY SHINING HOUR happened on a SUMMERTIME
was CHASIN' ANOTHER TRANE
'round CENTRAL PARK WEST
lost in LOCOMOTION
craving EVOLUTION
in search of SUNRISE
something OUT OF THIS WORLD
close
but far from the customary CONFIGURATION—
soul
funk
BESSIE'S BLUES
   (I'M OLD FASHIONED)

enter COUSIN MARY
   WISE ONE
   SUN STAR
comin' SOFTLY AS IN A MORNING
SUNRISE
AFTER THE RAIN
livin' the LUSH LIFE
she caught a SPIRITUAL/TRANE
and flew like a LAZY BIRD
to LIBERIA
and other STELLAR REGIONS
of the COSMOS
fled on a MOMENT'S NOTICE
ridin' the BLUE TRAIN
to ALABAMA
still
like EV'RY TIME WE SAY GOODBYE
she left an OFFERING
a SERAPHIC LIGHT
that shone a beautiful TAPESTRY IN SOUND
   CRESCENT
   LOVE SUPREME
AFRO-BLUE
I WANT TO TALK ABOUT YOU

'cause you put me IN A SENTIMENTAL MOOD
got me croonin' EQUINOX
LIKE SONNY
takin' GIANT STEPS
mind, BODY AND SOUL
croonin' that horn lick NAIMA sings

first IMPRESSIONS

and these are
    but a few of
        MY FAVOURITE THINGS

POETRY CAFÉ

I heard a word
when lips charted
a tale
the face could not
convey

the design left a taste
in my mouth
burning for the cayenne that fuelled the omen
the pep in the pepper
all/spice
and other communal season
bodies itching for reason
cram café corners and churn flavours from tongues
high hums and low drones
homegrown episodes
and far/away roams
breathed onto microphones
and peculiar crevices:

public washroom walls
tv commercials
elevators
storefronts
weathered roads

unleashing the load
of being
on a room full of
strangers—
many a mood

word of mouth
chart
high/life
on
shoestring
when
writers fed
food
for thought

the in-your-face-ness coasts delivery like rain to shower
the pulse of poetry streams minutes to hours

the word is heard
and rests
in the pocket of a poet
who totes
the note
she wrote
from finger
nails on broken skin
holding the fold of a page
a pencil end
and
for a season
picking up pieces of
matchless reason
to open the notion of
she

and he
crafts a motion
and we praise the poetry
he writ

"man u [can] script!"

raised high
in voices
fervent

poet's tree

   run rivers
     and nourish
       the current

T(HER)E

the smell of garbage is the air I breathe
a man's shadow haunts the place I call home
I want rest without the torment of dreams
an ocean calm away from sand and foam
I want
to go

go where fireflies dance like children

where the sun sets without number
and my feet have no concept of time

where the water is yellow with gold kisses
and crocs threaten geese with menacing eyes

where jesus birds walk on water
and silver fish scatter
where storks sidestep predators
and wild, unbridled horses graze without question
where my painted toes are out of place
and nature's palette boasts a potent display of indigo green
red rocks
orange
where time is immortal
and I am not (her)e
nor am I t(her)e
and I can find
refuge
   in large, open spaces
and discard
   days that hold me under
   gasping
I just want to breathe

breathe air
that tastes like strawberries
      red
      ripe
      and ready for picking

ART GALLERY

with art, there are no answers
only questions
ideas
perspective

not one thing replicated
each fibre: manufactured inside a fresh circumstance
each theory: born of a different mould
art is a puzzle
her pieces don't always fit

if they do
the consequence may cause you
to vomit
rip down the wall and reassign
each brick to a bold, uninhibited
crevice
a rebirth
    a newness

MUSING

to write
    when your mind is dancing
is to sleep
    with the world at your door

Scattering Jake
Yvette Nolan

CAST

Scattering Jake was first read at Diaspora Dialogues at Luminato Festival, Toronto, June 11, 2008, with the following cast:

DAVID: David Yee

NAOMI: Catherine McNally

DM: Cherissa Richards

YVETTE: Yvette Nolan

It received a second reading at Dis Place at Theatre Passe Muraille, Toronto, August 14, 2008, with the following cast:

DAVID: David Yee

NAOMI: Ruth Madoc-Jones

DM: Donna-Michelle St. Bernard

YVETTE: Yvette Nolan

ONE

DAVID, YVETTE, DM and NAOMI are standing in the yard of St. James Cathedral at King and Church streets. DAVID is carrying a man-bag.

DAVID: This is so illegal

NAOMI: we haven't done anything yet

DM: where is—he?

NAOMI: David's purse

DAVID: it's a man-bag

NAOMI: purse, man-bag

DM: at least you didn't call it his—

YVETTE: David's sac.

DM: Jeez!

YVETTE: you don't mind when I call mine my sac.

DM: that's because you—never mind—

DAVID: don't have one?

DM: *(putting fingers in ears)* la la la la la la

YVETTE: Sac is a perfectly acceptable name for it. Besides, I am saying *sac*, not sack. *Sac*, the French way. *Mon sac à dos*... my backpack.

DAVID: but so much more elegant.

YVETTE: exactly.

DM: this is not what we should be doing with his body.

NAOMI: It's not his body, it's his ashes.

DM: I am probably going to hell for this.

DAVID: More like jail.

DM: Jail?

DAVID: You can't just scatter human ashes anywhere. There are laws.

DAVID takes a cardboard box out of his bag and hands it to DM, who takes it and holds it gingerly. DAVID takes a package of cigarettes out of his sac and removes one.

NAOMI: I wish you wouldn't smoke.

DAVID: you and my mother

NAOMI: Don't you think it's disrespectful of Jake? Seeing as he—

DAVID: Died of lung cancer?

YVETTE: Technically, he didn't die of lung cancer

NAOMI: Hush

DM: *(weighing the box)* So light

YVETTE: He was this light near the end

NAOMI: Hush

YVETTE: Still, this is no way to finish the journey

DAVID: The journey? When did you get all—wise Indian?

YVETTE: always been Indian

DM: What did his people do?

DAVID: Who were his people?

NAOMI: We are his people, people. That's why we are doing this, why he asked for us to do this. 'Cause we are his people.

DAVID: Wow, that's sad.

NAOMI: That's not sad, it's an honour.

DAVID: No, there is no way when I died I would want me to be in charge of whatever ceremony or ritual or disposal

DM: Youch

DAVID: What? That's what it is...

NAOMI: You're not in charge, David, you're just—

DAVID: Here for comic relief?

NAOMI: No, comic relief is funny

DAVID: the dispassionate witness?

DM: Dispassionate?

DAVID: Unruffled, cool

DM: I know what it means, jackass. I just don't think you are
          dispassionate. I think you're just in denial.

DAVID: Denial? Of what?

DM: Of everything.

NAOMI: Alright, that's enough.

DAVID: No, I wanna know what DM means—

NAOMI: Well, this is not about you, David.

DAVID: Of course it is. Everything is always about me. How do I fit
          in this picture? Do I fit in this picture? How did I get in this
          picture?

YVETTE: Can I have a pair of scissors to cut myself out of this picture?

NAOMI: Don't encourage him.

YVETTE shrugs.

DM: Strangely, I don't think you are here for the picture, David.
          I think you are here for the words.

YVETTE: A thousand words maybe.

NAOMI: You're the chronicler.

DAVID: Why do I have to be the chronicler? Why can't Yvette be the
          chronicler? I'll turn it into fiction.

NAOMI: Yvette's not the chronicler this time. And she'll turn it into
          fiction.

YVETTE: Is that a good thing or a bad thing?

DAVID: What are you saying? That I don't make art? That I only
          document? That my writing is only so much public journalling?
          Now I think that I will kill myself.

DM: David, for god's sake, stop it! Stop making this about you.

YVETTE: Hush, he's just—we're all just—a little wrought. I think we are all feeling the responsibility, and it's scary.

DM: That's what she's here for.

DAVID goes to speak. YVETTE looks at him. He stops.

DM: How long?

NAOMI: A couple of minutes now.

DM: Maybe we should open the box.

NAOMI: Yeah, you're right.

DAVID: You haven't opened the box?

NAOMI: No.

DAVID: Well, how are we gonna divvy him up?

DM: What do you mean?

DAVID: Well, if we are supposed to put his ashes in four spots, shouldn't we divvy them up first? Or do we just open and shake, like Parmesan cheese, and kinda estimate what a quarter of the ashes look like.

NAOMI: I don't know.

YVETTE: Well, we better figure it out pretty quickly, because we are coming up on the hour and if we don't do it today, we'll have to come back tomorrow.

DAVID: I can't do tomorrow.

DM: Me neither, I moved everything from today to do this, my tomorrow is completely booked.

YVETTE: I am sure Jake will be fine if he isn't scattered right on the noon bells.

DAVID: You think?

YVETTE: No, I don't think. But I also don't think this is for him. Like I don't think he is hanging around watching us execute his last wishes. If he wanted to hang around, he—

NAOMI: Give me something sharp.

DM: Not your tongue

DAVID: Ha ha

DM: Not your head

DAVID: Ha fuckin' ha. I'm not packing

DM: Ha

NAOMI: Your pen, wiseass, give me your pen.

DAVID: Ah, you metaphor-maniac. Here.

NAOMI slices through the tape and opens the box. Inside is a plastic bag containing ashes.

NAOMI: Oh

DM: Oh what?

NAOMI: More plastic.

DM: Oh.

NAOMI: Time?

YVETTE: About thirty seconds by my watch.

DAVID: You'll wreck my pen!

NAOMI: I'll get you another

DAVID: It was a gift.

NAOMI: Oh for god's sake

DAVID: How am I supposed to chronicle if you wreck my pen? Here, give it.

DAVID rips the plastic with his hands, shakes the bag into the box.

DAVID: Now what?

DM: Yvette?

YVETTE: I think we should all take a handful. And when the bells start to ring, we should scatter the ashes to the four directions.

DAVID: This is so illegal.

YVETTE shrugs. She reaches into the box, takes a handful.

NAOMI: You gonna say something?

YVETTE: You want me to?

NAOMI nods.

DM: Cops. Cops. Slowing down. Oh shit.

DAVID: Well, don't look guilty.

DM: I can't help it! I'm black!

DAVID puts his arm around her neck.

DAVID: Look at me. DM. Look at me.

DM does.

DAVID: Look deep into my eyes.

DM looks at him.

DAVID: deep. like you mean it.

She does.

DM: Are they gone?

DAVID pulls her toward him and whispers in her ear. DM laughs.

YVETTE: Okay, they're gone.

NAOMI: what'd you say?

DM: Secret.

DAVID: The DM whisperer.

YVETTE: Right, everyone take a handful.

DAVID does. DM does, squeamishly. NAOMI just stands there.

NAOMI: I—I don't know—

YVETTE: It's okay, Naomi. It's all part of it. It's a good thing. This small
            good thing we are doing.

*YVETTE goes to her with the box. She takes NAOMI's hand, opens it,
puts some ashes into it, closes it.*

YVETTE: Our friend Jake loved this city, the dark alleys, the graffiti'd alleys—

DM: the theatres

DAVID: especially the theatres

YVETTE: he loved the bells of this church

DM: he loved this neighbourhood

DAVID: before it got all gentifried, pre-condo, pre-Starbucks

YVETTE: our friend Jake wanted to be put back onto the streets of the
            city he loved, back into the ground and the air and the water
            of Toronto

NAOMI: he said Toronto saved his life

YVETTE: and so we put all that is left of Jake back into the city, that he
            becomes part of the life of—

*The bells start to ring. YVETTE faces east and throws ashes. DM faces north
and flings. DAVID sprinkles west. NAOMI stands, lifts her fist to her face.
DAVID goes to her, puts his arm around her, takes her hand in his, faces south
with her. She opens her hand, turns it over, ashes fall.*

NAOMI: Pink.

DAVID: Yup.

NAOMI cries. DAVID holds her. YVETTE puts down something.

DM: Pink.

YVETTE nods.

DM: Who knew.

YVETTE: not me.

DM: what next?

TWO

DAVID, YVETTE, DM and NAOMI are standing on the ferry to Ward Island.
DM is hanging back.

DAVID: This is so illegal.

NAOMI: I don't think it is, David.

DAVID: There are rules. You can't just go scattering human remains
           any old place. Not into Lake Ontario. This is where they get our
           drinking water.

DM: Yum yum. That's why I don't drink tap water.

YVETTE: where do you think we go when they bury us in the ground?

DAVID: DM, why don't you join us?

DM: that's okay

YVETTE: are you afraid of the water?

DM: no

YVETTE: have you ever been on the ferry before?

DM: no

NAOMI: you haven't?

DAVID: DM, come here.

DM: it's okay, there's too much

NAOMI: too much what?

DM: nature

DAVID grabs her, holds her in front of him à la Titanic. *DAVID whispers to her. She laughs.*

DM: I'm flying!

NAOMI: maybe we should move further back to do this

DAVID: they shut down the Pirates of the Caribbean Ride at Disneyland because someone scattered someone's ashes in the water there

YVETTE: that's dumb

DM: who would want to spend eternity in a stupid theme park ride?

DAVID: either he really liked the ride, or it was revenge on his people

NAOMI: at least he didn't ask for a Viking funeral

YVETTE: why would Jake want a Viking funeral? Weren't his people English from way back?

DAVID: and American

DM: well, that would explain the Viking thing

YVETTE: what Viking thing?

DM: invaders, plunderers—

YVETTE: I thought he *didn't* ask for a Viking funeral

NAOMI: I'm sorry I brought it up

DAVID: hey, did you guys ever hear that story about Chocolate's Viking funeral?

DM: they had a funeral for chocolate?

DAVID: for a dog named Chocolate. Put him on a raft and set him on fire and set him afloat, right around here, I think...

YVETTE: that's gotta be urban myth

DM: I've always wondered how something can be both on fire and on water

DAVID: no really, someone wrote about it. I read it in—oh, *Geist*, I think

YVETTE: bless you

DAVID: ha. Anyway, it didn't work. I guess it didn't burn—

DM: see?

DAVID: —and a few days later commuters on the ferry were treated to the sight of the hairless, bloated corpse of Chocolate bumping up against the jetty.

DM: gross

NAOMI: David.

DAVID: Sorry. Sorry. Just trying to support you—

NAOMI: you're doing a fine job

DAVID: don't be sarcastic. That's my job. Or maybe DM's.

DM: I got nothing.

NAOMI: sorry. I—I'm finding this all—

YVETTE: yeah. *(beat)* You're doing good.

NAOMI: I thought it would be easier by now.

DM: Naomi, it's barely been a year. A year is not very long.

NAOMI: Thirteen months. But I've been fine. I've been good.

DM: yeah, you're doing great

DAVID: *After great pain, a formal feeling comes—*
            The Nerves sit ceremonious, like Tombs—

NAOMI: but I feel—I feel—*(touches her chest)*

YVETTE: okay, gang. I think it's time. David?

DAVID reaches into his sac and pulls out the box.

DAVID: careful now. Don't want him escaping before his time

NAOMI: I forgot about the wind. That it would be windy.

DM: yikes. Don't want him flying back in my face. No offence, Jake.

They each reach carefully into the box and take some ashes. YVETTE takes some tobacco from her pocket and adds it to her ashes.

YVETTE: Naomi?

NAOMI: no.

YVETTE: David?

DAVID shakes his head.

DM: Our friend Jake lived hard. He died as well as he could.
       God, we're only human. He was a good friend, a good artist,
       a good man. He loved life. He hated dying. Don't hold it
       against him, okay?

DM holds her hand out over the water and opens it.

DAVID: Very catholic.

DM shrugs.

DAVID: hey buddy *(opens his hand)*

YVETTE holds her hand to the sky, then over the water.

*They look at NAOMI. NAOMI nods, opens her hand. DAVID puts his arm
around her. The other two stand on either side of them, looking at the water.*

THREE

*DAVID, DM and NAOMI are walking with, variously, a picnic basket,
a cooler, a beach bag.*

DAVID: At least no one is going to freak out here

DM: why's that?

DAVID: 'cause they're island people, they're already freaky

NAOMI: they are not freaky.

DM: hey, I'm island people

DAVID: not Toronto island people. *(beat)* What island?

DM: Grenada. Do we get cell coverage over here?

NAOMI: ha ha

DAVID: I didn't know that. I thought you were from here.
          Like, Toronto born and bred.

DM: nope.

DAVID: wow. Grenada, eh? Operation Urgent Fury?

DM: Vikings.

DAVID: ah

DM: where is she taking us?

NAOMI: to the right place

DM: why can't this be the right place? It's got everything.
          Sand. Shore. Ducks. Those are ducks, right?

NAOMI: ducks.

DAVID: she's doing her faithful Indian guide thing

DM: it all looks the same to me. Why isn't this the spot?

YVETTE enters, carrying a basket.

YVETTE: This is good, I think.

DM: See? I knew this was the right place. Blankets?

YVETTE: yup

*From the bags appear blankets, tablecloth, and food in plastic containers.
They talk as they spread out the feast.*

NAOMI: Thanks for doing this. All of you.

DAVID: s'nothing

NAOMI: It's a lot. Taking the time to clear your schedules.
          Trekking around the city with me. All this.

DM: good reason to play hooky

NAOMI: I didn't know—who to ask—really. Seems like such
          a weird—quest.

DM: everything—about death—is weird, isn't it? You so rarely
do it, if you're lucky, so when you have to do it… *(beat)*
It was good of Jake to leave us such clear directions.

NAOMI: writing the script, choosing the locations, directing us.
Even in death.

DAVID: look at this spread. Chicken, salmon, potato salad, beans,
berries—

DAVID reaches to toward a container, DM smacks his hand.

DM: uh-uh. Feast. Gotta wait.

DAVID: oh. *(beat)* For what?

*DM shrugs, motions to YVETTE, who is collecting a little bit from every
container, putting it on a plate.*

YVETTE: plate for the spirits. For Jake.

DAVID: okay.

YVETTE: okay. Naomi?

NAOMI shakes her head.

YVETTE: David.

DAVID: I don't know how to pray. I don't know what I believe in.
I don't have any spiritual—thing.

YVETTE: you don't have to pray. You can just speak.

DAVID: *(beat) I will arise and go now, for always night and day*
I hear lake water lapping with low sounds by the shore;
While I stand on the roadway, or on the pavements grey,
I hear it in the deep heart's core.

           Jake was one of my first and best teachers. And here he
is a year dead, and still teaching me. I have lived in this city
all my life, but today, Jake is showing it to me anew. We live
on a lake. We *live* on a *lake*.

I learned a lot from Jake. About art, about words, about passion. I *didn't* learn a lot from him too, though he tried to teach me. About generosity, and humility, and compassion. I know I'm not supposed to say I wish he was here, but I do. I wish he was still here showing me stuff. I would be a better student.

DAVID stops. The others wait.

DAVID: Sorry. That's it.

NAOMI: That was good.

DM: Eat?

YVETTE: Eat.

DM hands them plates.

DAVID: I'm not hungry.

YVETTE: It's a feast. You have to eat.

DAVID: okay.

YVETTE: Come on, it's my famous roast chicken.

DAVID: The one with the lemons and sun-dried tomatoes and things—

YVETTE: yup

DM: *(piling food on her plate)* yum yum potatoes, yum yum beans

YVETTE: it's a feast for Jake, Naomi. We are feasting Jake.

NAOMI: I know. Okay, okay.

NAOMI begins to put food on her plate.

FOUR

Later that night, still at the picnic site. There has been a fire, but now it is embers. DM has a mickey of whiskey. She cracks it open and pours a bit on the ground, takes a sip, passes it to NAOMI.

DM: So what are you gonna do with the rest?

NAOMI: not sure

DAVID: you could make him into a diamond

NAOMI: what?

DAVID: sure, there's this company in the States that will turn the ashes of your loved one into a diamond

NAOMI: you're making this up

DAVID: nope.

DM: where do you get this stuff?

DAVID: it's everywhere. On the net, on the television. I'm a playwright. I am a student of the human heart. *(beat)* What?

DM: sometimes I can't tell if you're quoting one of your poets or if that's actually you speaking

YVETTE: wow. I guess people just need to do something—to memorialize —to mark the loving in some way—but that just seems so— wrongheaded—would you wear it?

DAVID: I guess that's the idea

YVETTE: seems like the opposite of what we are supposed to do—grieve —mourn—move on—live in the moment—how do you do that with your loved one there around your neck every day?

DM: or on your finger—like an engagement ring, *stay away stay away, I am spoken for, I am taken*

NAOMI: so the diamond idea is no

DM: no

DAVID: definitely no

YVETTE: yeah, no.

NAOMI: well, I guess that leaves eating him

DM: eeeyeww

DAVID: thanks, I am full of feast food

YVETTE: I'm down with that—DM? down with? Up with?

DM: down with, jeez

DAVID: you would? You'd eat him?

YVETTE: sure. Made sense to me in Heinlein.

DM: what's Heinlein?

DAVID: you don't grok Heinlein?

NAOMI: well, we've done concrete, water, sand

YVETTE: earth, air, water—

DAVID: I thought it was earth, wind and fire

DM begins to dance and sing.

DM: *ba de ya de ya de ya*

DAVID: wow, you know Earth, Wind and Fire?

DM: of course. C'mon, *ba de ya de ya de ya*

YVETTE: but not Heinlein

NAOMI: please don't make David sing

YVETTE: you can't make David sing. Or dance.

NAOMI: or quit smoking

DAVID: whoa, are we going back to picking on David? Not that I mind? I'd just like to know, so that I can gird my loins.

DM: gird your loins? Oooh *(hitting head)* get out! Get out!

YVETTE: you know, you don't have to decide right this instant

NAOMI: well, I sort of do. He said I would know. St. James at noon, the ferry to the island, the island, and then I would know what to do with the rest. Well, here we are. I've done my best, followed instructions, and here we are. Now what? Now the fuck what?!

Silence from the rest.

NAOMI: I don't know what to do next. I feel—like all this time—these
            months—I have just been going forward because that's what
            Jake expects, he expects me to go on, to keep working, to keep
            moving. It's what everyone expects, what'd you say? *grieve—
            mourn—move on.* And I didn't want to grieve too much, too
            publicly, because—We die, right? We live, we die, our friends
            do some rituals, some ceremonies, and life goes on for the rest.
            To grieve too much or too long is—unseemly. Especially for
            someone who cared less for his life than I did.

YVETTE: Naomi—

NAOMI: He smoked 'til he got lung cancer, which probably only beat
            cirrhosis by a few years, and then he didn't even have the
            guts to stick it out 'til the end. He didn't have the guts to fight,
            he didn't have the desire to stay with me—to stay a few more
            weeks or months—

            I guess I should be grateful he took pills and didn't blow his
            brains out.

            I am not grateful. I am angry. I am angry and I am abandoned.

            Nobody knows me the way he knows me. Knew me. I feel
            unknown now. No one will ever know me like that again.

            I feel like something is breaking up in here *(she touches her chest),*
            actually breaking—

*DM and YVETTE go to her, touching her. DAVID stands apart. He goes to
light a cigarette, then doesn't.*

DAVID: *This is the Hour of Lead—
            Remembered, if outlived,
            As Freezing persons, recollect the Snow—
            First—Chill—then Stupor—then the letting go—*

NAOMI: Yeah. Yeah.

YVETTE: See? That's why we brought David, he always has the right
            quotation.

DAVID: your own personal Bartlett's

DM: I can hardly wait to see what he writes from this.

DAVID: oh-oh, pressure.

DM: we have to give you a deadline, or else you'll never write—it. Whatever it is. What is it?

YVETTE: a poem

DAVID: no, I'm a terrible poet. That's why I memorize so many. Trying to figure out how they do it.

NAOMI: a piece for *Geist*?

YVETTE: bless you

NAOMI: Scattering Jake.

DM: a play?

DAVID: maybe a play. *Tragedy, comedy, history, pastoral, pastoral-comical, historical-pastoral, tragical-historical, tragical-comical-historical-pastoral, scene individable, or poem unlimited*

NAOMI: can you write it better?

DAVID: I'll try, Naomi.

NAOMI: okay.

DAVID: okay.

NAOMI: *(looking at her watch)* we should get going, if we want to get the next ferry

YVETTE: okay

DM: okay

They start to pack up. DAVID holds the ashes box.

DAVID: um, what do you want to do with—

NAOMI: oh, put it back in your purse

DAVID: it's a man-bag

DM: *(pointing at YVETTE)* don't even think of going there

YVETTE shrugs.

NAOMI: I don't have to decide right now.

DM: *(kicking at the fire)* you think this is out enough?

YVETTE: oh yeah, it's fine—

They pick up the bags and basket and cooler.

NAOMI: oh this is much lighter.

DAVID: that's because I ate an entire chicken and a pound of potato salad

DM: oh yeah, this is way better.

YVETTE: Come on, people. We don't want to miss the ferry.

As they exit:

DM: hey, David. Can I play me? In the play?

DAVID: sure I guess

NAOMI: I don't wanna play me.

DAVID: okay

NAOMI: okay

They exit.

ANAR ALI's work has appeared in various literary magazines and newspapers including *The New York Times* and *The Globe and Mail*. Her first book, *Baby Khaki's Wings* (Penguin, 2006), was a finalist for the Trillium Book Award, the Commonwealth Writers' Prize Best Book Award (Caribbean and Canada Region) and the Danuta Gleed Literary Prize. She was born in Tanzania, raised in Alberta and now lives in Toronto.

KEN BABSTOCK is the author of three books of poems, *Mean* (Anansi, 1999), winner of the Milton Acorn Award and the Atlantic Poetry Prize, *Days into Flatspin* (Anansi, 2001), winner of a K.M. Hunter Award and finalist for the Winterset Prize and, most recently, *Airstream Land Yacht* (Anansi, 2006), finalist for the Griffin Prize, the Governor General's Award and the Winterset Prize and winner of the Trillium Award for Poetry. Ken's poems have appeared widely in journals and anthologies in Canada, the United States and Ireland, and have been translated into German, Dutch, Czech, Serbo-Croatian and French. He lives in Toronto.

TANYA BRYAN is a writer and poet based in Toronto. She graduated from Journalism-Print at Niagara College in Welland, Ontario, and eventually moved on to make her livelihood behind the scenes in television after exploring other options in media and entertainment. She is currently working on a book of poetry for children.

MARIA CORBETT is an Irish writer and freelance journalist. She has a background in the arts and worked as an art curator for many years, including for the Bank of Ireland, one of the largest corporate art collections in Ireland. She has a bachelor of arts in sociology and art history from University College Dublin and a master of arts from the National College of Art and Design in Dublin. Maria's writing has included articles on Irish art, short stories and children's stories. She is currently working on a novel set in Toronto.

SHAUNTAY GRANT is a Nova Scotian writer, spoken word performer, broadcast journalist and musician. Her children's book, *Up Home* (Nimbus Publishing, 2008), portrays one of Nova Scotia's historic black communities. She is a founding member of Word Iz Bond Spoken Word Artists' Collective, which stages a monthly performance series in Halifax dubbed "SPEAK!" Shauntay has shared her blend of poetry and music throughout Canada as well as in Europe, the Caribbean and Australia, and her works have been featured nationally on CBC Radio, CBC Television and Vision TV. She also conducts arts workshops for youth and adults.

RAWI HAGE was born in Lebanon and immigrated to Canada in 1992. His books, *DeNiro's Game* (Anansi, 2006) and *Cockroach* (Ananasi, 2008), have been nominated for several awards, and *DeNiro's Game* won the 2008 International IMPAC Dublin Literary Award.

YIWEI HU currently attends the gifted program at Don Mills Collegiate Institute. She has been published in the e-zine *Writing in the Margins* and the magazine *Teen Ink!* After a stint in Tarragon Theatre's Young Playwrights Unit, she has developed a taste for writing plays too. She hopes to pursue creative writing as a career and, if not, languish in a law firm.

GUL JOYA JAFRI was born in Pakistan and raised in Toronto. She wrote her first story when she was six, and imagined she would be a writer when she grew up. Instead, she pursued a career working for the United Nations and the Canadian International Development Agency in Ottawa, Amman, Ramallah and Beirut. In recent years she has sought out ways to make time for her writing again and is enjoying the creative process. "Family Parade" is her first published story.

MARGE LAM, born in Coast Salish Territories, Vancouver, is a multimedia artist and community worker. Her practice of decolonizing the body and the land informs her work in poetry, radio and video. She has been published in *The Colouring Book*, a collection of writings by artists of colour, and, from this, in collaboration with the National Film Board of Canada, she created her first video short, *Unkept*. Marge has read at the Word on the Street Festival in partnership with Diaspora Dialogues, freelanced for CBC Radio One and CKLN, and co-hosted with Stark Raven at CFRO. She is currently making a home in Toronto.

JEN SOOKFONG LEE's first novel, *The End of East* (Vintage Canada and Thomas Dunne Books), was published in 2007 as part of Knopf Canada's New Face of Fiction program. Jen has appeared at a number of literary festivals and spoken at universities and high schools across Canada. She was the first debut novelist to be featured on CBC's Studio One Book Club and is now a regular on-air contributor to other CBC radio programs, including *On the Coast* and *Canada Reads 2009*. A founding member of the writing group SPiN, Jen lives and writes in Vancouver.

DANIEL DAVID MOSES is a Delaware from the Six Nations lands in southern Ontario. He holds an honours bachelor in general fine arts from York University and a master of fine arts in creative writing from the University of British Columbia. His plays include *Coyote City*, a nominee for the 1991 Governor General's Literary Award for Drama, *The Indian Medicine Shows*, a winner of the James Buller Memorial Award for Excellence in Aboriginal Theatre, and, his best-known play, *Almighty Voice and His Wife*. He is also the author of *Delicate Bodies* (Nightwood Editions, 1992) and *Sixteen Jesuses* (Exile Editions, 2000) and co-editor of the third edition of *An Anthology of Canadian Native Literature in English* (Oxford University Press, 2005). Daniel's most recent publications are *Pursued by a Bear, Talks, Monologues and Tales* (Exile Editions, 2005) and *Kyotopolis* (Exile Editions, 2008). His honours include the Harbourfront Festival Prize, a Harold Award and a Chalmers Fellowship and being short-listed for the 2005 Siminovitch Award. He teaches in the Department of Drama at Queen's University.

YVETTE NOLAN is a playwright, dramaturge and director. Born in Prince Albert, Saskatchewan, to an Algonquin mother and an Irish immigrant father and raised in Winnipeg, she lived in the Yukon and Nova Scotia before moving to Toronto. Her plays include *BLADE, Job's Wife, Video, Annie Mae's Movement*, the libretto *Hilda Blake* and the radio play *Owen*. She is the editor of *Beyond the Pale: Dramatic Writing from First Nations Writers and Writers of Colour*. In 2007–08, she was the National Arts Centre's playwright-in-residence. Currently the artistic director of Native Earth Performing Arts, Yvette was recently awarded the City of Toronto's Aboriginal Affairs Award.

SABRINA RAMNANAN was born in Toronto to Trinidadian parents. She completed her bachelor of arts in English and bachelor of education at the University of Toronto and is currently working toward her certificate in creative writing. Sabrina writes because of the wonderful tingly feeling it gives her, and because there is something thrilling about creating her own reality. Her poetry has recently appeared in *Cerulean Rain*. When she isn't writing, Sabrina can be found reading, teaching and dreaming in Scarborough.

PRATAP REDDY was born in India and moved to Canada in 2002. He is a financial analyst by day and a writer by night (to be more precise, the wee hours of the morning). He has completed a creative writing course from the Humber School for Writers. He writes short fiction about the agonies and the angst (and, on occasion, the ecstasies) of immigrants from India. In 2008 Pratap was awarded the Marty Award by the Mississauga Arts Council for Best Emerging Literary Artist.

ANTANAS SILEIKA is a novelist, magazine writer and occasional broadcaster. His last novel, *Woman in Bronze* (Random House, 2004), was a Globe Best Book. He is artistic director of the Humber School for Writers.

MOEZ SURANI's poetry and short fiction have appeared in numerous journals and anthologies. He has won the Kingston Literary Award, the *Dublin Quarterly*'s Poem of the Year and, most recently, a Chalmers Arts Fellowship, which will support a five-month research stint in India and East Africa. His debut collection of poems, *Reticent Bodies*, will be published by Wolsak & Wynn in the fall of 2009.

SANDRA TAM has published articles in newspapers, academic journals and magazines. Mainly she writes about gender and racial aspects of women's working lives. Sandra runs and cross-country skis when she is not working as a program and policy specialist with the Ontario Pay Equity Commission.

NAYA VALDELLON grew up in the Philippines, where she graduated with a bachelor of fine arts in creative writing from the Ateneo de Manila University and won a Palanca Award and a Maningning Miclat Award for her poetry. She came to Toronto in 2006 to take her master of arts in English and creative writing at the University of Toronto. She writes poems about the city, correspondences and loonies, and is currently working on a collection entitled "Open Letters."

Yarek Waszul was born in Warsaw, Poland, in 1980. When he was thirteen his family emigrated to Canada. In 2004 he graduated from the Ontario College of Art and Design and was awarded a Medal in illustration. He is based in Toronto and his work has appeared in many publications, including *Business Week, Maisonneuve, Mother Jones, The New York Times, SEED, The Walrus* and *WIRED*.

About the cover image:
"This picture is an attempt at describing a sense of dislocation and new identity forming in the space between spaces—a side effect of permanent migration/dislocation. It is a kind of moiré pattern of cultural and lingustic systems, and the effect those systems have on us. I capitalized on the visual resemblance of geography and topography to the anatomy of the nervous system to symbolize a psychological space and create a sense of erosion and mutation. I also used a floating linear composition to simulate a certain loss of orientation and the peripheral nature of these kinds of processes."

www.yarekwaszul.com

Diaspora
Dialogues

Diaspora Dialogues supports the creation and presentation of new fiction, poetry and drama that reflect the complexity of the city through the eyes of its richly diverse writers. Publishing and mentoring activities, as well as a monthly multidisciplinary performance festival, help encourage the creation of Canadian literature that is vibrant and inclusive, while bringing these works to a wide audience.

For information on programs, please visit www.diasporadialogues.com.

Diaspora Dialogues is supported by The Maytree Foundation, Ontario Trillium Foundation, Canadian Heritage, Ontario Arts Council, Canada Council for the Arts, the City of Toronto through the Toronto Arts Council, the George Cedric Metcalf Charitable Foundation and TO Live With Culture.